BETWEEN HISTORY AND LEGEND
STATUS AND POWER IN BUNDELKHAND

Between History and Legend
Status and Power in Bundelkhand

RAVINDRA K. JAIN

Orient Longman

The maps in this book are not to scale. The boundaries of Indian states and the external boundaries and coastline of India as depicted are neither authentic nor correct.

ORIENT LONGMAN PRIVATE LIMITED

Registered Office
3-6-272 Himayatnagar, Hyderabad 500 029 (A.P.), INDIA

Other Offices
Bangalore, Bhopal, Bhubaneshwar, Chandigarh, Chennai, Ernakulam, Guwahati, Hyderabad, Jaipur, Kolkata, Lucknow, Mumbai, New Delhi, Patna

First published 2002

ISBN 81 250 2194 9

Typeset by
Scribe Consultants
New Delhi

Printed in India at
Baba Barkha Nath Printers
New Delhi

Published by
Orient Longman Private Limited
1/24 Asaf Ali Road
New Delhi 110 002

To the memory of
My father, Shri Lakshmi Chandra Jain,
born in Bundelkhand
My teacher at Lucknow, Professor D.N. Majumdar
My colleague at Oxford, Professor E.E. Evans-Pritchard

Acknowledgements

Acknowledgements are due to:

A number of relatives and friends in Bundelkhand whom it is not possible to name individually. But I must single out for mention Shri Dashrath Jain and Shri Vinay Shankar (then Collector, Chhatarpur) for numerous contacts and insights in the field.

My daughter, Kajri, son, Shirish, and wife Shobhita, without whom this work would not have been possible.

To my typist Dharampal, who worked overtime.

And finally to Ms. Vidya Rao, my editor at Orient Longman, for her unstinting cooperation.

Some chapters in this book are revised versions of papers published earlier:

Chapter I is based on my paper, 'Bundela Genealogy and Legends' in J.H.M. Beattie and R.G. Lienhardt (eds.). *Studies in Social Anthropology: Essays in Memory of E.E. Evans-Pritchard* by his Former Oxford Colleagues. Oxford: The Clarendon Press. 1975. pp. 239-272.

Chapter II is based on my paper which bears the same title in *Economic and Political Weekly*, Vol. 15. No. 22. June 2. 1979.

Chapter V is based on a paper published in *Sociological Bulletin*. Vol. 26. No.1. March 1977.

Chapter VI is based on a paper published in *Relevant Sociology*. Vol. 9. No. 1. 1993.

Contents

Preface

Anderson has written that modernity—specially western modernity—drives 'a harsh wedge between cosmology and history' (Anderson 1983: 40). This monograph, consisting of previously published and unpublished essays now strung together in the form of a patterned text, is being offered at the junction of cosmology and history in social anthropology. When one ventures to study one's own society, the two questions raised by John and Jean Comaroff (1992) about ethnography and history collapse into one. Here the anthropologist is in the situation of one who is both 'in the game and out of it, watching and wondering at it'. Therefore, the zone between history and ethnography with cosmology as the overarching umbrella is a deliberate manoeuvre in this study: it is, if you like, an intimation of what are known as folk studies.

I believe that the crisis of representation in anthropology (Clifford and Marcus 1986) as it affects the native anthropologists calls for this manoeuvre. One need not apologise therefore for glossing over a good range of positivist ethnography and presenting instead the vignettes of folk conceptions analysed through the idiom and metaphor of the culture where they are located. Whether one calls this the dialogical approach or the scanning of narratives, the understanding is that continuity contains within it a design of metamorphic forces (Carrithers 1992). In other words, assembly, disassembly and re-assembly is what creates the so-called 'reality' as well as its textualisation. It is in this spirit that this book is being presented to a variety of readers and is open to numerous readings.

This book deals with both structure and history. Structure, structuration and de-structuration are here perceived as multiple dimensions of one and the same reality, and simultaneously as the author's handiwork. I also believe that substantially there is a twilight zone between the ancient and the classical textual history of India and the so-called archival present-day social history of contemporary times. This twilight zone is shadowed in the consciousness of the people, about whom one writes, through their legends and the supporting social structure. It is, therefore, a genre of history and ethnography which to my mind has not been explored separately from 'finished models' of structuralism (or any other 'ism'). I make no claims to holisms: this work is very much on the side of the fragment in this twist of the kaleidoscope.

Ethnographic data was collected during several fieldtrips from Oxford to Madhya Pradesh, northern India, during my tenure as Lecturer in Indian Sociology and Fellow of Wolfson College, Oxford University, from 1966 to 1974. I am grateful to the Board of the Faculty of Anthropology and Geography, Oxford University and to the Fellows, Wolfson College, for grants enabling my travel between UK and India. A Visiting Fellowship at the Indian Institute of Advanced Study, Shimla, facilitated fieldwork during 1968-70. My thanks are also due to the Wenner-Gren Foundation for Anthropological Research for a grant. I received valuable advice and criticism from my colleagues at Oxford, especially R. Needham and the late John Beattie. The imperfections of the work are, of course, my own.

School of Social Sciences R.K. JAIN
Jawaharlal Nehru University
New Delhi
31 July 2001

CHAPTER I

Bundela Genealogy and Legends: The Past of an Indigenous Ruling Group

Introduction

Until a year after the independence of India in August 1947, the northern districts of Madhya Pradesh formed the territories of native states ruled over by the scions of Rajput (literally 'kingly sons' from the Sanskrit *Raja-putra*) families. From the beginning of the nineteenth century, the British had established their paramountcy over the native states. This chapter deals with the traditional history of these native kingdoms (*rajya* or *raj*) as rendered in the oral narratives and endogenously written sources of this area. More specifically, my concern here is to demonstrate the value of these sources in defining the region of dominance and salient social institutions of a ruling group known as the Bundela. The area of the former Bundela kingdoms is still known by its indigenous name 'Bundelkhand' (literally, 'the domain of the Bundelas'). It might also be mentioned that besides designating the territory of former Bundela rule, Bundelkhand is the name of a linguistic region of India. The great majority of the people of four southern districts of Uttar Pradesh and eight northern districts of Madhya Pradesh speak Bundeli, a dialect of western Hindi. The Bundeli linguistic

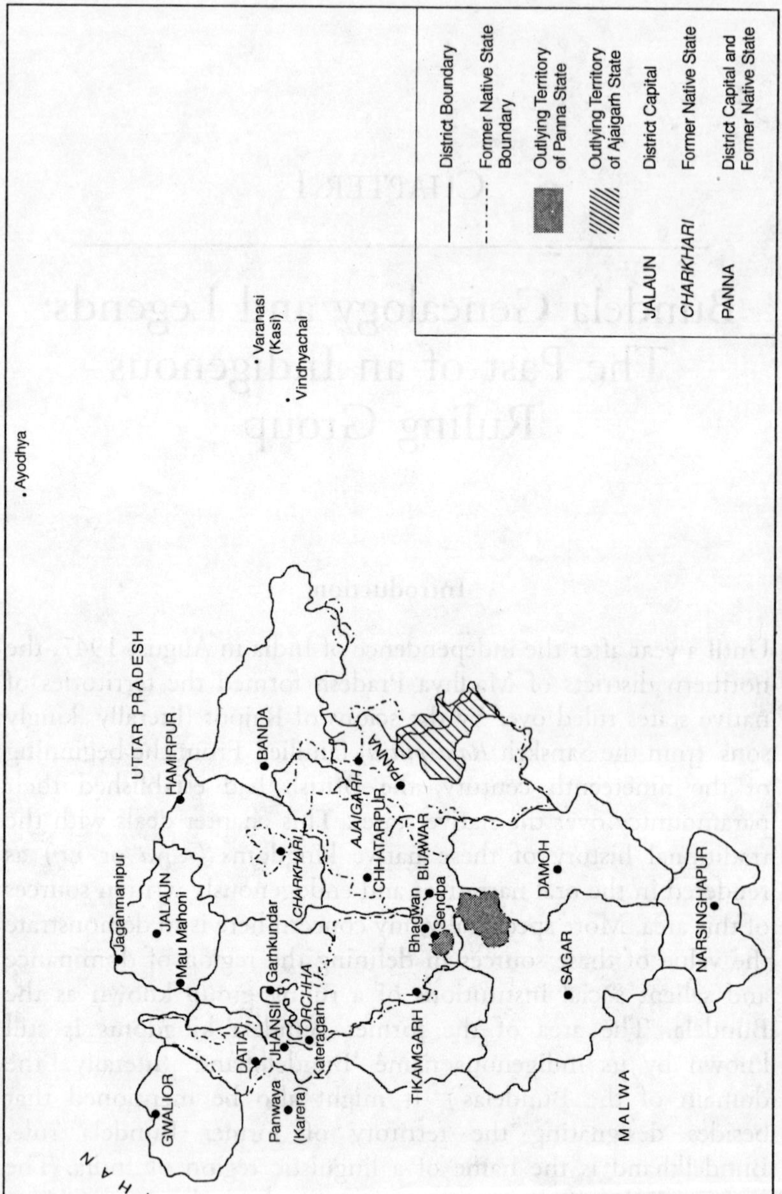
District Boundary
Former Native State Boundary
Outlying Territory of Panna State
Outlying Territory of Ajaigarh State
JALAUN District Capital
CHARKHARI Former Native State
PANNA District Capital and Former Native State
Ayodhya
Varanasi (Kasi)
Vindhyachal
UTTAR PRADESH
HAMIRPUR
BANDA
JALAUN
Jaganmanipur
Mau Mahoni
CHARKHARI
Garhkundar
ORCHHA
JHANSI
DATIA
GWALIOR
Panwaya (Karera)
Kateragarh
TIKAMGARH
Bhagwan
Sendpa
BIJAWAR
CHHATARPUR
AJAIGARH
PANNA
DAMOH
SAGAR
NARSINGHAPUR
MALWA
RAJASTHAN

Fig. 1

region is much larger (43452.4 sq.km) than the area of the former Bundela kingdoms and domains (22180.7 sq.km).

The data was collected in the course of intermittent fieldwork, from 1969 to 1971, in several villages and towns of Chhatarpur district in northern Madhya Pradesh. Present-day Chhatarpur has been carved out from the territories of former Bundela kingdoms including, of course, the kingdom of Chhatarpur itself. Chhatarpur had been ruled over by the descendants of a Panwar chieftain who had, until 1785 AD, been a retainer in the army of the Bundela raja of Panna (thus the hybrid 'Panwar Bundela' as the 'caste' of the Chhatarpur dynasty in official records). Besides Panna, the other Bundela kingdoms surrounding Chhatarpur were Orchha, Datia, Charkhari, Bijawar, and Ajaigarh. Orchha was the parent Bundela kingdom, founded c.1501 AD. The kingdoms of Datia and Panna separated from Orchha in 1626 and 1657 AD respectively. Charkhari, Bijawar, and Ajaigarh were formed from Panna territory in the second half of the eighteenth century, following dissension amongst the descendants of Maharaja Chhatrasal (1649-1731), the founder of Panna.

Bundela Genealogy

The most comprehensive charter for the Bundela past is their genealogy (*vamsavali*). It is a record of a strictly exogamous patriline. When put into diagrammatic form, it shows only males descending from males. The women are not represented.

Histories compiled from primary or secondary sources—in Hindi and English—provide succession lists of the ruling dynasties. The ruling line is the main or senior line. These sources also contain lists of subsidiary or junior lines, since all descendants of the ruling stock (*rajya vamsa*) were normatively included among the right-holders (*haqdar*) in the kingdom. Since such lists could become unwieldy, only those agnates from junior lines that possessed large hereditary appanages (*jagir*) in the kingdom have been selected. Those marital allies that held appanages in the kingdom are also listed. A typical example is the compilation in the series *Rulers, Leading Families and Officials in the States of Central India* (Calcutta and Delhi, 1911-41).

At present, the most senior living member of a Bundela patrilineage in one village or a group of nearby villages, usually possesses an up-to-date genealogical extract of his own residential unit (*patti*). This local group corresponds to a minimal segment of the Bundela patriline. The apical ancestor for this segment would be the Bundela founder of the *patti*. Nevertheless, the term *patti* denotes a share. It implies division from a larger entity and segmentation of the group from a higher level. The definition and scale of customary rights to a share are validated at this higher pre-*patti* level of segmentation with reference to those areas of the genealogy where a local Bundela patrlineage is linked by descent to a particular ruling house. This indigenous procedure of tracing rights among rural Bundela landholders was imperfectly understood by the British, who intervened in their land-disputes throughout the nineteenth century. The discrepancy between Bundela custom and the alien juridical framework which the British attempted to enforce on local Bundela dominants (*thakurs*), is epitomised in the repeated assertion by the latter that they were co-sharers (*hissedar*), and not merely right-holders (*haqdar*), in certain Bundela kingdoms. This does not deny the existence of customary law by which the distribution of rights, offices, and titles over territory in the indigenous kingdoms was regulated. It merely establishes a strong linkage between Bundela customary law and Bundela rules of descent, succession, and inheritance—the sphere of 'family law' as Maine saw it—and the problems in attempting to align it with substantive law through a 'double institutionalisation of custom' (Bohannan, 1965:34-37).

The Bundelas had a vested interest in emphasising their common descent from their rulers. This is reflected in the ability of Bundelas in rural areas, to trace, beyond the *patti* level, their patrilineal links with the ruling dynasty of the kingdom where they are located. Since all Bundela kingdoms grew by a process of political fission in the patriline, the links between various ruling dynasties are also contained in Bundela genealogy. As mentioned earlier, historically the Bundela dynasty of Orchha was the parent ruling house from which the other Bundela kingdoms subsequently separated. The last Bundela kingdom thus formed, was Charkhari. The *patti* level of Bundela patrilineal segmentation, designated here as the dominance level of Bundela genealogy, is thus subsumed by the dynastic level which spans—socially and politically—the time and space of kingdom formation in Bundela history.

However, in the genealogy itself the origin of the Bundelas and their kingship, (as distinct from historical kingdoms) belongs to a legendary and mythical past. The legendary and mythical levels of the genealogy are an invaluable repository for the anthropologist and can be explored for the unconscious structure of Bundela ideology of descent-based rule. The view of their past depicted at these levels exercises a powerful hold on the popular imagination of the people of this area. This is expressed in a variety of media—stories, songs, poems, and anecdotes. The Bundelas themselves enact their legendary origin in the annual ritual worship of the Devi (the female principle in divine creation). The categories of Bundela rule—the boundaries of socially legitimate exercise of power by the ruling group—are constituted by the formal and sensory properties of symbolic statements and enactments associated with this legendary and mythological past. An analysis of the myths and legends of Bundela origin and kingship in the next section of this chapter, demonstrates that these levels of Bundela genealogy, (like the dominance and dynastic levels), do not stand in isolation. They form an integral part of encapsulated history of the ruling group represented as a hierarchical series. Before the analysis, however, two clarifications are necessitated.

The myths and legends of Bundela origin have a dual aspect. The legends trace Bundela descent from an eponymous apical ancestor and, at the same time, describe the origin of Bundela kingship in the present territory—the region of the Vindhya mountains. With regard to the specificity of geographical information, the legends of Bundela territory identifying it with the Vindhya mountains, stand between the much clearer geo-political boundaries of the kingdoms described by dynastic histories and the elemental and transitive sacred geography of their mythology. The association of the group with a more or less specific territory is one criterion for distinguishing the legendary from the mythological. The latter, in the absence of an unequivocal territorial specification, should be viewed as the standard 'great tradition' prolegomenon to Hindu royal genealogies.

The second clarification concerns the analytical vocabulary adopted in discerning the patterns of descent at various levels of Bundela genealogy. So far the terms 'patriliny' for the genealogy as a whole, and 'local patrilineage' and 'royal house' for territorially identifiable groups corresponding to the dominance and dynastic levels of Bundela genealogy have been used. The term 'patriline' is a translation of the indigenous *vamsa.* Owing to the segmentary structure of Bundela unilineal descent groups, however, the same term, *vamsa,* may occasionally be used to denote a smaller unit, e.g. a 'local patrilineage' and a 'royal house'. But in a context where the smaller units need to be distinguished from more inclusive descent constructs (for example, the patriline as a whole), the terms *kula* and *khandan* are used interchangeably. Among the terms denoting a more inclusive descent construct for the Bundelas, the indigenous *kuri* and *bans* belong to the same semantic set as *vamsa*. Lexically, *bans* is a corruption of the Sanskrit *vamsa.* In the written genealogies of Bundelkhand, the Sanskrit word *vamsa* is invariably employed to designate the record as a whole (genealogy-*vamsavali*), and in the mythological aspect of the genealogy, for example, to designate the two main branches—solar (*surya vamsa*) and lunar (*chandra vamsa*) of the ruling (*kshatriya*) clans. However, from the legendary level downwards, the unilineal descent segments, (not only of the Bundelas but of their 'Rajput' marital allies as well), are designated as *bans.* In spoken Bundeli, moreover, the term *bans* is uniformly employed to designate Bundela genealogy as a whole (*bansavali*), the mythological branches, and the 'Rajput' clans(e.g. Bundela *bans*).

The most common designation for Bundela corporate identity and the last of these meanings is inherent in the speech of the Bundelas, viz., in the expression 'The Bundela clan is not a friend of brothers' (*Bundela bans bhaiyya ka mit nahin hota*). I locate the meaning of *bans* as clan at the legendary level of Bundela genealogy. In my definition, the Bundela *bans* is a clan in that all Bundelas trace their mythical descent, through males, from an eponymous ancestor; through him they identify themselves with a more or less specific territory; and they practice *bans* exogamy. It corresponds to the maximal level of segmentation of the Bundela patriline.

Closely allied to the ideas of *vamsa* and *bans* (but much more complex) is the term *kuri*. The most frequent local usage of this term suggests a classification of Rajput *bans* into two categories along an East-West territorial axis. Each category is endogenously known by the number of clans composing it. There are, therefore, the 'three-kuri Rajputs' (*tin kuri ke Rajput*), and the 'thirty-six-kuri Rajputs' (*chattis kuri ke Rajput*), belonging to the eastern region (Bundelkhand) and the western region (Malwa and Rajasthan), respectively. Here, the term *kuri* is being used in its meaning of 'kind' 'type', or 'variety' (Hindi *prakara*). The translation is provided by the informants themselves. But the term '*kuri*' as used this way, does not, by itself, suggest a basis for classifying Rajput clans into these two categories. Nor does an ancillary usage which sorts individual Rajput men of families as belonging 'either to the three of the thirty-six' (*tin me ke, ya chattis me ke*) tell us any more than that being different from one another each category represents a unity of some kind.[1]

A second meaning of the term *kuri* is more explicit. A Hindi lexicon (*Nalanda Visal Sabdasagar*) gives the following meanings: '[noun, masculine gender] (In Sanskrit), i.a grain, bean sprout, (In poetry), vamsa, gharana, khandan, (In Desaja), a plough, [noun, feminine gender]; (in Hindi), a subdivision, a part, a portion.'

Undoubtedly the term *kuri* is a derivative from the Sanskrit *ankura* which means 'sprout', 'blade', 'hair', 'water', 'blood'

(Monier-Williams, 1964:7), In this semantic set the term *kuri* is a metaphor for the segmentary ideology of Bundela descent. The Bundelas themselves express the idea of fission and fusion of their patriline in a statement about the process of the formation of segments (e.g. a local patrilineage): 'formerly all were one, subsequently different *kuri* sprouted' (*pahle sab ek the*; *bad me alag alag kuri phut gayin*). *Kuri* in this statement, and in many similar statements, is associated with 'sprouting'. Similarly, with reference to a particular apical ancestor or brothers, it is said that from him or them, 'the branching-out commenced' (*phutan chali*). Here the apical ancestor—always male—is likened to a seed. An apt graph of the collective representation of the Bundela patriline in the metaphor of sowing and sprouting is the genealogical extract, characteristically drawn in the form of a creeper or a plant, with the male descendants only being shown as leaves on several veins and the leaves again sprouting more leaves on more veins. The orientation is always bottom upwards.

As handled in speech by my Bundela informants, the term *kuri* connotes both the fission and fusion aspects of Bundela patrilineal descent ideology. Yet, the principle of patrilineal segmentation cannot be extended to the classification of Rajput clans (including the Bundela clan), into the 'three-kuri' and 'thirty-six-kuri' categories without further exploration of the internal structure of each category. I hope in this exploration the identification of the exogamous 'clan' segment at the legendary level of Bundela genealogy will prove serviceable. The grounds for an experiment in Bundelkhand ethnology are provided by the fact that the eastern or Bundelkhandi category (the 'three-kuri Rajput') can be identified with three exogamous clans, viz. the Bundela, the Panwar, and the Dhandhera. Intermarriage among the three follows a rule of non-hypergamous circulating connubium. However, in one legend, the Bundela conquerors are depicted as having consciously formed a league of intermarriage with the other two groups, following help rendered by them in their victory against an out-group, the non-Kshatriya, Khangar. Thus martial alliance preceded marital alliance. Here is a perfect case of two structures which, as comparative social anthropology tells us, interpenetrate each other — on the one hand, 'political' and, on the other, 'descent and alliance'. My limited purpose here is to clarify the terms of this juxtaposition on the basis of the Bundelas' view of their past.

The Myth of Royal Origin

The mythical beginning of royal Bundelas has a typically Hindu character. The account starts with Lord Visnu (Narayan, reclining on the serpent, Sesa who holds the universe). From Visnu's placenta, in the form of the stem of the lotus flower, issues Brahma. From Brahma issues Marichi. From Marichi is brought forth Kasyapa. By Kasyapa's wife, Aditi, are born the eldest son, Surya (the sun), and the gods (*devata*); of his twelve other wives, by Diti are born the demons (*daitya*). The descendants of Surya (*Suryavamsi*) are Iksvaku, Dilip, Raghu, Aja, Dasaratha, Ramachandra, and the two brothers, Lava and Kusa. Lava becomes the ruler of Punjab. Kusa succeeds to the throne (*gaddi*) of Ayodhya. The descendants of Kusa are Haribrahma and Vihagaraja. In the seventh generation, Vihagaraja's descendant is Kiratdeva. A few generations after Kiratdeva, Virabhadra, the Raja of Kasi (Benaras), is descended. The Bundelas, in this version, are the descendants of Virabhadra through the line of his younger son, Hem Karan, alias Pancham, alias Jagdas.

This mythical prologue contains elements which carry a symbolic significance at all levels of royal-descent ideology and for Bundela genealogy as a whole. The origin of the rulers from the stem of the lotus flower is one such element. On account of its free-floating roots, the lotus flower is a persistent cosmological Hindu motif for depicting the exalted origins of royalty (Bosch, 1960). It symbolises the special creation and inherent legitimacy of kingship, investing royal descendants with the spiritual authority which they must possess as lords and protectors of 'land-cum-people'.

Secondly, in the oral tradition, Bundela kings are descended from the sun (*Surya*) and belong to the solar pedigree

(*Suryavamsa*). The conjunction of the sun and the lotus is regarded by the Hindus as auspicious. Both these, and their related attributes, have occupied a significant place in Bundela symbolism of kingship, e.g. in royal architecture. Thirdly, demons and gods are brothers as Kasyapa's sons. While the idea of brothers as potential enemies permeates Bundela royal agnation, the principle of succession by primogeniture is clearly expressed in specifying that Rama's elder son, Kusa, succeeds to the throne of Ayodhya. Finally, kingship is associated with sacred geography. Only two capitals, Ayodhya and Kasi, are identifiable places. Both have multiple associations with the Hindu sacred tradition. Along with three other pilgrim centres they belong to a quintet of sacred Hindu locales. As a 'great tradition' mode of classification this quintet, rather like the fourfold *varna* scheme, serves to legitimise kingship in the idiom of descent.

The flexibility inherent in associating royalty with sacred locales has been exploited by genealogists to insert fictions of glorious antecedents for their Bundela patrons and by priests and poets to align the royal pedigree with their own priestly pedigree. A good example of the latter is an early seventeenth century poetic biography of the Bundela ruler of Orchha, composed by his brahmin priest and poet Kesava Das.[2] Kesava Das, whose own ancestors came from Kasi, constantly refers to his Bundela royal patron by the honorific 'Kasi Raja' (the Ruler of Kasi). The title did not conform to the historically known boundaries of the kingdom of Orchha, which never included Kasi (Benaras or Varanasi in modern Uttar Pradesh). The point here is not that Kesava Das was fabricating Bundela history; rather, on account of its sacredness in Hindu ideas, Kasi, like Ayodhya, is a good place to think of as the seat of royalty.

The Legend of Bundela Origin

The legend of Bundela origin narrated to me in Sendpa village is as follows. Virabhadra, the king of Kasi, had two queens. From the senior queen (*patrani*) there were four sons; Raj Singh, Hansaraj, Mohan, and Man. The son of the second queen (*lahuri rani*; literally, junior queen) was Jagdas, alias Hemkaran. Following Virabhadra's death, the half-brothers of Jagdas refused to give him a portion (*hissa*) in the kingdom of Kasi and banished him. Jagdas wandered away to the shrine of Vindhyavasini Devi (literally, 'the Devi who dwells in the Vindhya ranges') to do penance under her protection. ('Devi' is the manifestation of the female principle in divine creation; when not regarded as a deity localised in the Vindhya mountain ranges she is known by her generalised name 'Devi', or by any of her other manifestations as 'Bhawani', 'Durga', 'Kali', etc.) Despite the most arduous penance, he received no sign of blessing from the Devi. Dejected, Jagdas decided to offer his life in sacrifice to the Devi by beheading himself with his sword. No sooner had a drop (*bund*) of blood dripped onto the floor from a cut in his throat, than the Devi appeared and held the hand of her devotee. She blessed him with the boon that from that drop of blood a brave son who would conquer large territories to be known the world over as Bundelkhand would be born.

With a few variations and additions of detail the same legend appears in an eighteenth century poetic biography of Maharaja Chhatrasal, the Bundela ruler of Panna, composed in his life-time by the poet (*bhat*), Lal Kavi or Gorelal. In this text (Lal Kavi, c.AD 1700) the name of Virabhadra's son from the second queen alone is mentioned. He is called Pancham or Devadasa. Both these names are formulaic in the sense that they refer to the attributes of the person being designated; Pancham means 'the Fifth'(his place in the sibling birth-order) and Devadasa, 'the deity's servant' (his disposition for acquiring a boon from the goddess). Although the text is far from explicit, it seems to indicate that Virabhadra, in his own lifetime, partitioned his estate (*puhumi* meaning 'land'; it might also stand for 'kingdom') among his sons. Pancham being a minor, Virabhadra, as father and king, became the trustee of his share of inheritance. Following Virabhadra's death, Pancham's four older brothers grew covetous, took advantage of his minority, and appropriated his portion of the estate 'partitioning it among themselves in four shares'. There is no mention of Virabhadra's successor to the seat of Kasi. This makes sense if we bear in mind the mythical character of this 'seat', and my view that the story of Pancham marks the point of transition from a mythological to a legendary level of Bundela past.[3]

The forward-looking facet of the legend, which enables us to view Pancham as the founder of the Bundela clan, is his gaining a kingdom and a patriline of royal descent after being gifted a heroic son by Vindhyavasini Devi. Pancham's son was created from a drop of Pancham's own blood and appropriately called 'Bundela' (from *bund*—drop). Details of the boon, given in the gift (*varadan*) of a son to Pancham, and the son's 'special creation' by divine interposition, are vividly portrayed in the poem. The mental process by which Pancham, the unhappy prince, is drawn towards Vindhyavasini Devi is known as '*yoganidra*' (which Pogson renders as 'Jog Nidruh'), 'the tranquil repose of the mind from an abstraction of ideas' (Pogson 1828: 6). Pancham practices penances and austerities at her shrine in Vindhyachal, the hills near Mirzapur in Uttar Pradesh, and a neighbouring religious resort on the Ganga. The episode is narrated as follows in the text:

> After the first seven days Pancham heard a voice from the sky say to him, 'Your land will be restored to you.' He replied, 'I have practiced these austerities to win your [Devi's] favour.' Whereupon, the voice returned to the sky. Somewhat heartened by this, he devoted the next seven days to even stricter penances and gradually lost all hope that his wish would be fulfilled. He took out his sword and poised it to behead himself in sacrifice to the Devi. However, by now his perseverance, piety, and devotion had won her affection. She appeared in person and wrested the sword from his hand. Drops of blood oozed out from a few gashes on his head, 'like stars shooting from the sky'. The sight filled her heart with pity. She instantly conveyed to the wound some *amrita*, or water of immortality, inherent in every *devta*. At the same time *amrita* rained from the sky. A drop of Pancham's blood which fell on the ground assumed the form of a child, a replica of Pancham. On beholding the infant, she [Devi] was filled with maternal affection and put it to her breast, which supplied a copious flood of nourishment. Then,

> blessing Pancham and the baby, she, with prophetic spirit, revealed that the sword should always help him in war, and be the prop of his prosperity, by which the sovereignty should continue from one generation to another... 'Thou, O favoured mortal,' she added, 'shalt repossess thy estate, increase them to the full extent of thy wishes and conquer all against whom thou wagest war.' Then placing her hand on his head, she said, in commemoration of the drop [*bund*] of blood, 'Thine descendants shall be called Bundelas'.

In this version the conjunction between the principle of descent and territory in the Bundela ideology of kingship is expressed in the metaphor of divine intervention in human affairs (the *pauranic* device). In reality the Vindhyas are a mountain range. The territory and the female principle dwelling there take their name from it. In the metaphorical structure of the legend Vindhyavasini Devi represents 'territory-for-kingdom.' She is actually designated *puhumi* or 'land' (fem.) in the course of the poem. Bundela, the son created from a drop of Pancham's blood on the earth, is nourished by Vindhyavasini Devi—the divine female principle—blessed by her with a line of brave royal descendants; and is gifted away to Pancham. This son incarnate is to be distinguished from Pancham's other, 'real', son Bir Bundela. The former never again makes an appearance in the book. What remains of him is only the name 'Bundela' assumed by Pancham himself after the incident, and passed on to his descendants. The son incarnate is, therefore, a ritual apotheosis of the principle of clanship at the legendary level of Bundela genealogy. All Bundela royal houses worshipped Vindhyavasini Devi as their clan goddess (*kula devi*), although the members of Bundela lineal segments, localised in rural areas, worship their clan goddess in her generalised form, Devi. What is significant about the legend of Bundela origin is its representation of territory in the form of Vindhyavasini Devi endowed with multi-vocal symbolic significance—the female principle, the territory, and the giver and nourisher of princes. Through her divine intervention unilineal descent (blood) and territory (milk) complete the picture of Bundela royal agnation in the idiom of clanship (*bans*).

A Legend of Bundela Expansion

The expansion of the Bundela clan following the boon to Pancham is closely associated with the legendary martial exploits of his royal descendants in the Vindhya region. One particular event, again the founding by conquest, of a separate kingdom by one of the royal siblings, is repeated extensively in all oral narratives and receives significant mention in literary works as well. The following summary is based mainly on the latter set of sources: Arjanpal, ruler of Mahoni had three sons: Birpal, Sohanpal, and Dayapal. Sohanpal was a most capable warrior. He reduced the forts of Garhkundar and Kateragarh.[4] Sohanpal undertook the successful expedition to Kateragarh on behalf of his father. His victory at Garhkundar followed the death of his father and his elder brother's succession to the throne of Mahoni. The cause of this expedition was Sohanpal's dissatisfaction with his share of inheritance. With forty-five sepoys and thirteen sowars, Sohanpal went to Naga (alias Hurmat Singh), the Khangar raja of Kundar, seeking his help in taking his share from his brother.

Naga promised to help him, on condition that Sohanpal eat, drink and intermarry with him. Sohanpal was enraged at this suggestion, and was about to leave Kurar [Kundar], but hearing of his intention, Naga formed a plot to forcibly detain him and compel him to accede to his proposal. Sohanpal hearing thereof, fled from the court, and went to Mukatman Chauhan, a descendant of Dhandhera Deva who commanded 4,000 men on behalf of Naga. He requested his assistance against his brother, but Mukatman refused, saying that he would remain neutral. After this, Sohanpal, leaving his small force behind, went alone successively to the Salingars, Chauhans and Kachwahas, and told them his story. But none of them offered to assist him. However, a Panwar Thakur named Panpal (Punyapal), Jagirdar of Karhara, offered assistance, and together they conspired to remove Raja Naga from his kingdom, the revenue of which was worth 13 lakhs. It was agreed that Sohanpal should go to Kurar and pretend to accept Raja Naga's conditions of intermarriage, etc., and invite the raja and his relations to his house. Sohanpal went to Kurar and, after a time, Raja Naga, his brothers and ministers, came to Sohanpal's house, whereupon Panpal arrived with 300 Kshatris. As soon as Raja Naga and his followers sat down to eat, Panpal Panwar and Sohanpal Bundela fell upon and slaughtered all the Khangar chiefs, and immediately seized the fort of Kurar. In this way, on Wednesday, the 2nd of Kartik Sambat 1354 (1288 AD), Sohanpal became Raja of Kurar and appointed Panpal and Mukatman as his ministers. He said to them, 'As no Kshatri in my time of distress gave me help except you, no other save yourselves shall marry into my family.' Accordingly, he gave his daughter in marriage to Panpal and as dowry a village named Itaura, and to Panpal's younger brother a *jagir* of one lakh. From this time the Kshatris were divided into three different classes of Bundelas, Panwar and Dhandheras. The total revenue of the whole Bundela territory was 26 lakhs of which half, Birpal possessed, and the rest was Sohanpal's. (Silberrad op. cit.: 105-106.)

This is the most secular of early Bundela legends. It depicts two social processes which must be kept conceptually distinct in order to understand the political expansion of Bundela rule in the Vindhya region. The first is a process of caste segmentation. Luard (1909:15), Tiwari (1933:118-22), and Archival Records (B.A.R., 1905, 48/51) contain information about the natal clans of the wives of Bundela rulers from Bir Bundela to Sohanpal (Fig. 2 p. 16) which confirms that before the capture of Garh Kundar, the Bundelas intermarried exogamously with a large number of Rajput clans. The marriages of Sohanpal's immediate descendants, on the other hand, take place with the Panwar and Dhandhera clans only. Tiwari further hints that the narrowing of the Bundela endogamous circle involved their exclusion from commensal relations with the other Rajput clans. Similarly, there is evidence that the Panwar and the Dhandhera had also experienced exclusion from a more inclusive Rajput category. The views of nineteenth century amateur historians (Elliot 1869: i.45; Smith 1881:1-52; Franklin 1827:259-81), attributing inferior or impure Rajput status to the Bundela, on account of

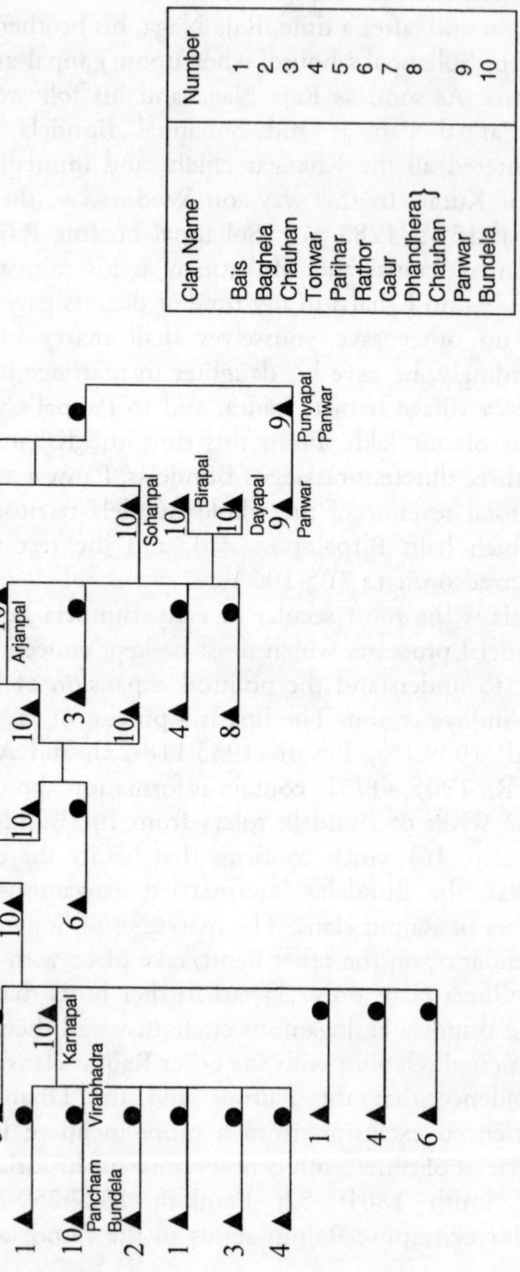

Fig. 2 Bundela and their marital allies from Pancham to Sohanpal

miscegenation with the non-Aryan Khangar, could also be seen to describe a process of caste segmentation by exclusion.[5] Whatever the specific terms under which this process is perceived, the concept of caste segmentation emphasises the relative hierarchy of statuses among the Rajput. In this particular case an endogamous segment of the main body of Rajput caste, formed by a process of exclusion, had a definitely lower ritual status vis-a-vis the rest.

What is excluded from the main body of Rajputs constitutes the inclusive category, the 'three-kuri Rajput'. The constituent units of this category are three intermarrying exogamous clans. The discrete groups belonging to the three clans are localised lineage segments. The principle of inclusion, I submit, cannot be elucidated by the process of caste segmentation, but only through the complementary processes of dispersed clanship and merging lineage segmentation (Fox 1967:122-31).[6]

In our exploration of these processes, we encounter the Bundela legend of expansion not in its function as a cover for social and ritual exclusion, but as a charter of social and political inclusion. The contextual information in our sources elucidates this function.

Rajput territorial organisation in much of insular central India during the pre-Bundela period was based on dispersed clanship. Each named clan (*bans*) was an exogamous unit. Its constituent patrilineages at various levels of segmentation were designated, in addition to the clan name, by the locality (a village, or cluster of villages) where the relevant apical ancestor is supposed to have created rights in land and its produce either by conquest or political alliance. These rights tended to become presumptive. Thus, even when they were overlaid by superior rights, say through conquest by another clan or by a foreign power, or during the protracted absence from the locality of members of the original descent-group, they could still be revived, if the occasion warranted. Their non-recognition by the authorities became a frequent cause of rebellion, (cf. Malcolm 1824: i.508-11) on the rights of the Grassia chiefs; Sleeman 1915: 245-52) on the '*bhumia*' of Bundelkhand; also, Irfan Habib

1963: ch. v for central India during the Moghul rule). This customary claim, (whatever be its historical character), by deep patrilineages to particular territories, formed the basis of their local identification. Legends of former rule by the concerned clans, which still abound in these localities, are probably not without some historical foundation, as long as alleged dynastic succession is distinguished from agnatic inheritance of presumptive rights in land and its produce, and a fully fledged state political system is distinguished from a combination of feudal and acephalous political systems.

The various localised patrilineal segments of Rajput clans referred to in the legend of Bundela expansion can be set against the background of social and political organisation delineated above. They were located in the Gwalior-Jalaun-Jhansi region, roughly the same area as Arjunpal's seat of Mahoni. The various chiefs who exchanged women in marriage appear to have been *primi inter pares* as dominants (*thakurs*) in their localities. The diversity of titles assumed by them either emanated from their position in the segmentary lineage structure stratified into senior and junior branches (e.g. *rao*, *diman*, and *sawai diman*) or they referred to offices held currently or in the past in a local patrilineage as feudatories to a superior power (e.g. *raja*, *rai*, and *diwan*).

The power equality of chiefs or dominants in the regional political system on the eve of the Bundela conquest of Garhkundar at the end of the thirteenth-century A.D. is vividly portrayed in a historical novel (Verma 1956). Hurmat Singh, the Khangar ruler of Garhkundar, (a descendant of Khet Singh), was appointed governor of the region after Prithviraja Chauhan's victory over a former Chandela ruler (c. A.D. 1182). After only a decade of overlordship, Prithviraja was defeated by the Muslim invader, Shahabuddin Ghori. For the next 100 years or so, the line of Khangar governors, even though divested of representative authority derived from a superior power, maintained some kind of suzerainty over regional Rajput dominants.[7] By the time Hurmat Singh became ruler, repeated Muslim invasions had created chaos in the wider political arena and left the regional political system completely acephalous. In order to gain political advantage through territorial expansion, the local lineage segments of Rajput clans arranged and rearranged themselves into patterns of marital and martial alliance.

Interpreting the formation of the 'three-kuri Rajput' from the legend of Bundela expansion, one must distinguish between martial-cum-marital alliance in the context of the regional, social, and political structure and the message concerning the superiority of the kshatriya ruler vis-a-vis that of the non-kshatriya Khangar. The former cannot be wholly understood from merging lineage segmentation, nor the latter merely as caste segmentation in the idiom of ritual hierarchy. What is the middle ground left, in historical fact and conceptualisation, between these dominant modes of interpretation? The answer suggested by a contextual interpretation of this Bundela legend has, as I shall point out in conclusion, wider implications.

The lineage organisation of ruling clans at this time had an important political function. The Khangar ruled over the wild tracts of south-eastern Bundelkhand by allocating political authority to localised lineage segments, where each segment was identified with a fortress serving as a military garrison. Fortresses assigned to rulers' sons as secondary capitals continually figure in Bundela legends and in traditional history as well. Conflict between half-siblings in the Bundela ruling lineage of Mahoni is presaged by a military expedition commanded by Sohanpal to capture the fort of Kateragarh. According to Bundela annals (Silberrad op. cit.: 105), besides being overlooked in the succession, Sohanpal was disinherited of this fort. It is conceivable that this disinheritance was the main cause of the quarrel between him and Birpal. In later Bundela history it became a standard tactic for a ruler to assign a fort far away from the capital to a troublesome younger brother. As later research (Drake-Brockman 1909:188) has shown, Kateragarh is not the southern fort of Silberrad's account. It was located far too close to Mahoni for Birpal to assign to Sohanpal.

However, the agnatic factionalism in the ruling lineage, which was an important cause of Sohanpal's expedition against the

Khangar, does not, even according to the legend, lead to permanent fission. The fate of the senior branch (Birpal-Dayapal), after Sohanpal's capture of Garhkundar, is not passed over. The breach between the half-siblings is healed but on terms dictated by Sohanpal. There is an equal division of territory between him and Birpal, while Dayapal is assigned an appanage (*jagir*) of one lakh. This is an early example of the process of merging lineage segmentation in the Bundela ruling group. The idiom in which this merger is expressed is that of kingdom (*rajya* or *raj*) but we have no need to assume that it refers in this case to a centralised state political system.

The legend tells us that a connubial league of the Bundela, the Panwar, and the Dhandhera was formed following their martial alliance to defeat the Khangar. But it is not clear why this inclusive category, the 'three-kuri Rajput' covers all Bundela and not merely Sohanpal and his descendants? There is no indication whatever (either in Bundela history or in present-day practice), that some Bundela, viz. the descendants of Birpal and Dayapal against whom the martial league was partly directed, were excluded from the marital league. Conversely, no section of the Bundelas has shown consistent normative preference for marriage with the Rajput of thirty-six kuri and a corresponding disinclination to intermarry with the Panwar and the Dhandhera. It would be easy to 'explain' the exhaustive inclusion of the Bundela into the 'three-kuri' category by evoking the superior and contagious efficacy of ritual exclusion over political alliance: the well-known phenomenon of the formation of sub-castes. This, precisely would be the argument of those analysts who assume that the dynamics of inclusion and exclusion in Indian social structure has to be based on the ritual hierarchy of purity and impurity. In this case, however, it is the historical and contextual facts of changes in the distribution of political power that explain the dynamics of social structure. To be more precise, we move away from a model of caste-based dynamics to one based on the clanship of Rajput groups in this region. Thus, to the extent, however, that there are deep localised patrilineages of the Bundela Rajputs in the Bundelkhand region, a long history of kingdom formation and rule by Rajput branches from the mid- fifteenth century to the mid-twentieth century, and the lack of a consistent hypergamous pattern of marriage in the three-kuri Rajput 'caste', the framework of intra-caste ritual hierarchy is by no means self-evident. Correspondingly, explanations of socio-political organisation in terms of ritual hierarchy, or inclusion and exclusion, (for example, caste-segmentation), do not work automatically, i.e. outside time. These social facts demand that analysis take a different direction. The internal dynamics of lineage organisation bears a structural relationship to its external political function. In the case of Bundela lineages, during the period of their expansion, the organisational framework of their external political functioning is dispersed clanship.

The political implication of this dispersed clanship, are better understood by specifying the internal and external functioning of patrilineages in clans allied to them by marital and martial bonds during the capture of Garhkundar. The clans directly involved are the Panwar and the Dhandhera, but the Chauhan, the Tonwar, and other clans belonging to the category of the 'thirty-six-kuri Rajput' also enter the picture. Punyapal, to whom Sohanpal gave his daughter in marriage, belonged to a Panwar patrilineage in Gwalior. The Panwar of Gwalior enjoyed a high rank among the regional Rajputs, taking brides from the eastern Chauhan dominants (Sherring 1872:165) and the Tonwar rulers (Luard 1907:16). Punyapal's father had received the appanage of Panwaya in dowry from the Tonwar ruler of Gwalior, whose daughter he had married. We have no comparable data for appanages and offices held by the affines of Bundela rulers at Mahoni. From the fact that during this period the Bundela are constantly shifting their capitals southwards, it is possible to speculate that the quest of Bundela heroes, of 'territory for kingdom', pervades the entire legendary phase culminating only in the founding of their first dynastic capital at Orchha in c.1531 AD. With their victory at Garhkundar, however, we begin to hear about appanages and offices granted by Bundela rulers to their affines. In developmental terms, the Bundelas at this juncture enter the cycle of kingdom-formation in which the Tonwars of Gwalior had already attained maturity.

The story of Punyapal Panwar strikingly reveals the link between marital and political alliance in the Rajput cycle of kingdom formation. At the same time it throws up certain geopolitically conditioned contrasts[8] between the social organisation of dominance between the 'three-kuri Rajput'(the eastern division) and the 'thirty-six-kuri Rajput' (the western division). According to a legend, Punyapal Panwar had a horse which his uncle (mother's brother), coveted. This horse, he agreed to give to his uncle in exchange for a beautiful dancing-girl. On the appointed day he went to his uncle's house mounted on the horse. As he rode up he saw the dancing-girl standing among the people surrounding his uncle. Without waiting to make a saluation even, Punyapal rode up to the girl, swung her onto his saddle, and followed by his people, galloped home. Insulted, his uncle, it is said, persuaded all the Rajputs to have nothing to do with Punyapal's family. (Luard 1907:16.)

The broken exchange between the mother's brother (the Tonwar ruler) and the sister's son (the Panwar 'vassal') expresses a political conflict in the kin-feudated Rajput polity of Gwalior. In Rajput legends of Bundelkhand, the gift of a concubine's daughter frequently symbolised the value given in exchange by the ruler to a political ally. Translated into quasi-jural terms, the gifted woman represented some kind of subordinate territorial rights granted to an ally by the ruler(cf. Kanhaiyaju 1928: 169-208, for an example concerning Chhatrasal and the Peshwa). The horse, on the other hand, represented the oath of martial fealty by a Rajput 'vassal' (*jagirdar*), to his politically superior kinsman. An exchange that involved a Rajput's parting with his favourite horse might seal a political alliance between kinsmen or ritual kinsmen; such a transaction did not extend to non-kin, even though the party proposing the transaction was the paramount ruler himself (Sleeman 1915:182).

According to the legend, as a consequence of the broken exchange, not only the Tonwar, but also other Rajput clans that had marital and political links with the Panwar, stopped interdining and intermarrying with the 'family' of Punyapal Panwar. Unlike the Bundela, this exclusion applies only to the Panwar patrilineage of Panwaya; the western Panwar patrilineages (such as of Malwa) continued to intermarry with the 'thirty-six-kuri Rajput'. Punyapal Panwar of Panwaya, the head of the excluded family, married the daughter of Sohanpal Bundela, who gave him the appanage of Karera in dowry. Thus included among the eastern or Bundelkhandi 'three-kuri Rajput', Punyapal Panwar becomes the apical ancestor for localised segments of Panwar patrilineage of Bundelkhand.[9] In political terms, Punyapal replicates the career of his father; he establishes the same kind of political-cum-affinal link with Sohanpal Bundela as his father did with the Tonwar ruler of Gwalior.

In relation to the exogamous Panwar, then, the process of exclusion (of a section from the 'thirty-six-kuri') is marked by asymmetry of ritual status,[10] but that of inclusion (of a section into the 'three-kuri') is characterised by the symmetry of political forms. The former process lends itself to conceptualisation, both by the observer and the observed, as an occurrence in mythical time. The latter process is remembered in legends of territorial expansion and political incorporation.

Just as Panwar and Tonwar constituted a special alliance in the regional set of intermarrying Rajput before the Bundela capture of Garhkundar, so also the Dhandhera and Chauhan are depicted as special allies. The Dhandhera claim to be the descendants of Dhandhu, an officer in the army of Prithviraja Chauhan (Drake-Brockman 1909:92). This is the martial link. The marital link with the Chauhan can be inferred from the description of Mukutman Chauhan, master of an appanage of the Khangar of Garhkundar, as 'a descendant of Dhandhera deva… which probably means that he was Dhandhera on his mother's side' (Drake-Brockman ibid.: 92-93). Mukutman Chauhan has also been depicted as *matul* (classificatory mother's brother) of Sohanpal Bundela (Verma op. cit.: 25). He chose to remain neutral in the quarrel between the Bundela brothers. It is likely that Sohanpal's avuncular relationship with Mukutman derived from 'linked affinity' between the regional

Bundela, Dhandhera, and Chauhan patrilineages. Insufficient information is available on the local identification of intermarrying lineages, but there is enough to indicate that the Dhandhera only *gave* their daughters to the Chauhan and Bundela.

Does this suggest the ranking of these intermarrying patrilineages in a hypergamous pattern? Sherring, writing about the Chauhan of the Banaras region (the eastern Chauhan), speaks of a pattern of directional hypergamy. The western Panwar are included among the wife-takers of the Chauhan, but the Bundela and the Dhandhera are not mentioned either as givers or takers. Bundela sources, on the other hand, suggest that the Bundela rulers of Mahoni and Jaganmanipur were Chauhan wife-takers, which contradicts the supposed rule of exclusively northern (and western) hypergamy among eastern Chauhan. The Chauhan of the Sagar region (southern Chauhan) are discussed by Russell and Hiralal, who report the breakdown of clan exogamy and the formation of Chauhan sections into territorially endogamous sub-castes. As a system of sub-castes the Chauhan developed a ritual hierarchy of marital unions—the products of unequal unions being assigned to an appropriate status-gradation. The offspring of unequal Chauhan unions would perpetuate the status inferiority of their birth. The matrifilial identification of Mukutman Chauhan with the Dhandhera would seem to belong to this system. It is in terms of the operation of this system that we may also explain the identification of the Dhandhera of Sagar region (southern Dhandhera) as an offshoot of the Panwar clan (Russell and Hiralal 1916: iv: 148, 439). Since the Panwar and the Dhandhera of the Bundelkhand region intermarry, it is obvious that the southern Dhandhera had branched off from the western Panwar. Therefore, there is a structural homology between the Chauhan and the Panwar. In both cases the clan is subdivided into localised branches (thirty-five in each case), some of which cluster in territorial endogamous and hypergamous sections of sub-castes. The Bundelkhandi branches of the Panwar and Dhandhera fall outside the framework of clans transformed into castes. The lack of internal status gradations regulated by hypergamy in these branches indicates the strength of clanship among them.

The clanship of the Mahoni Bundela, which provided leadership for the capture of Garhkundar, clearly constitutes the pivot for the political incorporation of their martial and marital allies into the 'three-kuri Rajput' division. Unlike their Panwar and Dhandhera allies, the principle of Bundela clanship emerges untrammelled by any claims to a previous connection with the clan-caste configuration of the 'thirty-six-kuri Rajput' division. As constituted in the ideology and traditional history of Bundelkhand, the 'three-kuri Rajput' division has shown no tendency for internal hierarchical segmentation. The western Rajput tendency to transform the exogamous clan into caste, converts in the east into territorial expansion and political consolidation by kin-feudated kingdom formation.[11]

It is vital to distinguish between the political function of clanship and the ritual function of caste (*jati*) as an idiom of hierarchical status distinctions. The typification of hypergamy as characteristically 'Rajput' in Indian sociological literature (Rivers 1921; Dumont 1966:116-23) rests on a confusion between these two functions. It will not do to simply state that the ritual function of *jati* subsumes the political function of clan. What I am contending in the context of Bundelkhand is the absence of a necessary and sufficient interdependence between the attribution of ritual status by *jati* segmentation and the processes of political power which in the cases of the 'three- kuri Rajput' category, developed, changed, and atrophied by the principle of clanship. The reason why a distinction has not been maintained between the two functions and why, in discussions of Rajput hypergamy, the political functions of descent have been reduced to manifestations of ritual status hierarchy is not hard to seek. The cultural premise, 'Rajput hypergamy par excellence', is based on one variant of the conscious model, that provided by the western-Rajput division, which has so far been studied to the exclusion of other regional modalities. A few indigenous Rajput scholars have complained against this bias in the work, for example, of Tod (cf. Sengar 1927:1049).

A more serious deficiency in Indian sociological literature emanates from the elaboration of an 'unconscious' model from one variant of the conscious model. The 'truth' of this partly observer, partly observed model of hypergamy as an entailment of hierarchy is beyond doubt, but the model takes account only of mythical time. To the extent that historical time is excluded from it, a simplified equation between hierarchy, caste segmentation, and hypergamy of the indigenous ruling groups hinders, rather than helps, the perception of key variables in the social organisation of dominance. This, in any case, holds good for the Bundelkhand region during the pre-British period. I seek to doing more than just putting the historical record straight. It would seem that the residue of institutionalised conflict in nineteenth-century central India leading up to the currently publicised contemporary menace of 'dacoity' (brigandage) in Gwalior and Bundelkhand cannot be understood without restoring to their legitimate place the ideology and processes of clanship in the traditional ruling groups.

The Clanship of the Ruling Group

We can see how the regional Rajput ideology of kingship contributes to kingdom formation by transforming the Bundela martial alliance with the Panwar and Dhandhera into a marital alliance. The symbolic equivalence of 'territory for kingdom' with the female principle, as contained in the legend of Bundela origin, is conducive to the formation of a territorial state based on a confederation of three Rajput clans that exchange women. For the dynastic and dominance phases of the Bundela past there is much evidence to suggest that the form of their polity was defined by processes of kin (including affinal) dispersal and merger. The legendary phase enables us to view these processes delimited by the symbolic constraints of exogamy and alliance as aspects of the ideology of clanship in the ruling group.

Clearly the principle of clan exogamy alone is insufficient to explain all the available facts of political and affinal incorporation involved in Bundela expansion and kingdom formation. Why should the connubial league of the ruling group be confined to three 'Rajput' clans? What prevented the Bundela from intermarrying with the non-Rajput Khangar, as amateur anthropologist-historians speculated they actually did? The answer would seem to lie in the operation of the ideology of legitimate rule derived from the attributional category (*varna*), kshatriya. Indigenous sources consistently oppose the kshatriya Bundela and other 'Rajput' clans to the Khangar as non-kshatriya. As the myth of royal origin specifies, the appurtenances of legitimate rule belong only to those who are born kshatriya. Nevertheless, as noted earlier, the same myth also sacralises territory. It serves as a cover for the uncertain possession of actual territory by the 'kingly-sons'. Now, the insertion of the territorial equation into the attributional category, kshatriya, is manipulated by the notion of royal clanship. In accordance with the rule of royal-clan exogamy, a kshatriya clan might give and take daughters (or have political agreements over territory) with the other kshatriya clans, but not with the non-kshatriya. Hence the absolute refusal of Sohanpal Bundela to have connubial and commensal relations with the Khangar.

In relation to the vanquished Khangar, the Bundelas' kshatriya role, as rulers protecting 'territory-cum-people', is narrated in an oral version of the legend of Garhkundar:

> Maharaja Sonhanpal led an expedition to Garhkundar and killed all the Khangar men who had gathered in the fort. He spared their women, since it is forbidden for the kshatriya to kill women. One Khangar woman hurled her new-born son at Sohanpal's feet and begged for mercy. Her wish was granted and the baby was spared. But from then on it became the bounden duty of the Khangar to be the 'shoe-bearing servants' (*naquib*) of Bundela rulers. (Narrative from Sendpa village.)

The descendants of the Khangar boy were incorporated into Bundela polity. They functioned under the general title *khasbardar* as aides-de-camps to Bundela rulers. The Khangar tradition recorded by Luard (1909:10-11) corroborates the story of their political incorporation as *khasbardar*: Luard notes that it became a hereditary title for the Khangar of Ath garhiyawal families (see note 7) employed by Bundela royals as petty officials. Furthermore, the nature of this conflict between the kshatriya and non-kshatriya is underscored by the symbolic significance of a set of restrictions imposed on the Khangar by the Bundela victors. The Khangars were not permitted 1. to wear red turbans; 2. to touch *kathris* (swords); 3. to drink liquor; 4. to put red lead on their hair-parting; 6. to eat *rotis* (baked bread) sold in public; 7. to eat *kachchi* (boiled food) touched by a kshatriya, vaishya, or shudra (Luard op. cit.: 11). These restrictions cannot be understood simply as defining a low ritual status for the Khangar in the caste hierarchy; they are precise ritual diacritics confirming the loss of political power and pretensions to royal prerogatives now legitimately wrested from the Khangar by the victorious Bundela as kshatriya. Again the system of social stratification of the ruling groups of the 'three-kuri Rajput' category seems supported by rituals which do not fit neatly into a theory of caste-segmentation operating in mythical time. They appear rather as creations conjoint with political developments in historical time.

Finally, we broach a question which has evoked considerable controversy among scholars, namely, Rushton Coulborn's contention (1968:371-72) that the kinship idiom as recorded by Tod in Rajput polities of nineteenth-century Rajasthan is a cover for weakened feudal relationships of medieval India. Richard Fox has correctly reversed the terms of Coulborn's contention (Fox 1917:135-38). By delineating the full developmental cycle of Rajput lineage in North India, Fox attempts to show that the political role of kinship might appear weak in the later stages of the lineage cycle, but among regional communities of Rajput dominants throughout pre-industrial North India, there always existed a potential for kinship solidarity to re-emerge and initiate a new cycle of lineage-based dominance. 'Genealogical categories', says Fox, are like phosphorised halloween costumes. The sun may set on the interactional political fortunes of local corporate kin bodies, but the largely attributional categories of lineage, clan, caste, and varna would continue to glow eerily as luminescent reminders of what once had been. (Ibid.: 171.)

Fox regards 'lineage, clan, castes, and varna' as attributional categories of the same order—manifestations equally of 'super stratification'. In so far as he lumps together the various denotata of 'Rajput' ideological unity, Fox's case, like that of many previous scholars, rests on positing a functional equivalence between hypergamy among the unilineal descent-based Rajput groups and the processes of caste- segmentation in the non-Rajput *jati*. The case of the 'three-kuri Rajput' category of Bundelkhand, supported perhaps by Mayer's discovery of a lack of conscious ideology of hypergamy and a weakly developed unconscious practice of 'directional hypergamy' among the Rajput of Malwa (Mayer 1965:29, 210-11), raises serious questions on the applicability of Fox's generalisation for the Rajput of central India.

Fox admits that his understanding of Rajput clanship, in the crucial issue of defining the boundaries of exogamy and endogamy, is inadequate. Thus, for example, his data for north India is inconclusive as regards the endogamy of various 'lineages of recognition' claiming to be related by Chauhan clanship (Fox op. cit.: 41). As I have shown, our sources for the Rajput of the central (Malwa and Bundelkhand) and eastern (Banaras) regions suggest a distribution pattern, along a broadly west-east axis,[12] which fits with the indigenous classification of Rajput clans into bunches of thirty-six and three. Both these patterns are constituted by the complementary principle of caste and clan. Based on the relative dominance in each pattern of one or the other principle, they may be formally classified as caste-clan (western)and clan-caste (eastern). The Chauhan or Panwar 'branches' in the first pattern belong to an endogamous or hypergamous system, while those of the second, retain an emphasis on clan exogamy. Indigenous political development in pre-industrial northern and central India would also seem to be governed by the varying modalities of these two patterns.

In a final example, we note that the expanding Bundela rulers received constant military support from the Ahir cattle keepers. The Ahir groups of Bundekhand, like their namesakes in other parts of north and central India, belong to a well-known caste-category which ranks lower than the Rajput. Similar to their affinal alliance with Rajput clans and political incorpoation of the Khangar, the Bundela rulers forged a link of pseudo-agnation with the *Yadu bansi* Ahir in the ritual idiom of clanship through 'the line of milk'. The 'milk brotherhood' between the three Bundelkhandi Rajput clans and a regional section of the Ahir, called the 'Dauwa' has frequently been noted in nineteenth- and early twentieth-century literature. In all the historical accounts and legends collected by me in villages of the Chhatarpur and Tikamgarh districts, this special relationship of Bundela rulers with the Dauwa is connected with their conquest and settlement in the Vindhya region. While the Ahir men—who came to be designated *dau* (father's elder brother) by the Bundela princes—provided the fighting militia, their wives as wet-nurses (addressed and referred to as *day-ma* or *dudh-ma*; literally, 'milk mothers'), nourished the princes with their own milk. It would take me far beyond the scope of this discussion were I to link this practice with the royal-clan exogamy of the 'three-kuri Rajput'. It is enough to note that the pseudo-agnatic incorporation of the Dauwa, not only with the Bundela, but with the Panwar and Dhandhera as well, furnished an ideological solution to the breach of the incest taboo created by restricted exogamy and the repeated affinity of the 'three-kuri Rajput'.[13] As to the ideological rationalisation of the special relationship there are two versions; one, relates the Dauwa as 'brothers' generally to royalty and the other, particularly to the Bundela-Dauwa alliance.

The first version was given to me in the form of a legend by the Bundela residents of Bhagwan village.

Once the daughter-in-law of Indra (the king of gods) prayed to Lord Visnu. The Lord appeared in the garb of a beggar and demanded her amputated breast in alms, which she offered without a moment's hesitation. The Lord was pleased and asked her to name a boon. She wished Him to be born as her son. This the Lord granted, saying that she would be born as Nandini and her husband as Nanda. He would then be incarnated as Krishna in Gokul and suckle at her breast. The Dauwa are the progeny of Nanda and Nandini.

Veena Das, in a paper on the caste *purana* of Gujarat (Das, 1968), has shown the miraculous appeal of Krishna as the epitome of kshatriya ideals in validating the claims of a wrestler-brahmin caste to a confirmed brahmin status in *Kaliyuga.* Here too, Krishna, the reincarnation of Lord Visnu, is the divine prince but unlike the brahmins of Gujarat, the Dauwas' special relationship with rulers is not mediated by brahmin priests but by the symbolism of the breast and its metonym, milk. Furthermore, the myth is enacted in the ritual practice of Dauwa women suckling royal princes, and the foster relationship is institutionalised by the elaboration of an appropriate kinship terminology.

The second version is derived from *Chhatraprakasa.* It pertains to the mythical origin of Vindhyavasini Devi, the tutelary deity of the Bundela. It will be recalled that in recounting the legend of Bundela origin, Lal Kavi, the author of *Chhatraprakasa*, refers to a mental process known as *yoganidra* by which Pancham is drawn to the shrine of Vindhyavasini Devi. In the text of the poem the same mental process appears deified as the prior aspect of Vindhyavasini Devi identified with the uterine daughter of Krishna's foster-mother Nandini or Yasoda (Pogson op. cit.: 6-7). According to the *Devi Bhagwat Purana*, Kansa, the ruler of Mathura, had decided to kill his sister Devaki's, son, Krishna, as soon as he was born. The Devi, as Yoganidra or Yogamaya, decided to be born as Yasoda's daughter who would be exchanged for Devaki's son (Krishna) in order to protect him from Kansa. Krishna and Yoganidra are born at the same time from the wombs of Devaki and Yasoda respectively. The exchange having been successfully accomplished, Krishna survives as the foster-son of Yasoda, while Kansa prepares to kill

Yoganidra, Yasoda's daughter, in Devaki's possession. As soon as she is hurled against a rock to be killed, Yoganidra assumes her real form as Devi and rising to the sky utters the curse of Kansa's eventual death at Krishna's hands. Then she retires to dwell in the Vindhya hills as Vindhyavasini Devi.

The Ahir, as *Yadu bansi*, trace their descent from Nanda and Yasoda. On account of the myth of their fosterage by the couple, they regard Krishna, and his brother Baladeva, as *Yadu bansi* as well. The myth of the Devi is shared by all Hindus of Bundelkhand, including Ahir and Rajput groups. For these groups however, the Krishna episode in the mythical cycle of Devi (*Devi Bhagwat Purana*) provides an excellent rationalisation for claiming a special relationship in the idiom of descent. Thus, Vindhyavasini Devi as the Bundelas' tutelary deity, represents 'the line of milk' and is symbolically identified with the female principle and the territory for rule; for the Ahir, though unconnected with territory, she is the uterine daughter of their progenetrix, Yasoda. The insertion of the territorial equation in their descent ideology of clanship enables the Bundela at once to retain a premium on kingship, and yet to exploit the allegiance of the Dauwa as foster-brothers. The ritual suckling of Buṇdela princes by Dauwa women is in conformity with this symbolic conjunction.

Conclusion

An unfortunate consequence of using caste as a blanket term for all hierarchical status distinctions has been to obliterate the perception of other contextually meaningful schemes of classifying political and social relations. Thus if we do not freeze the ruling groups' descent in a caste framework but examine it in the context of the expansion of indigenous rule, we can discern at least three bases of political relations between the ruling groups and their allies in Bundelkhand: intermarriage (Bundela-Panwar-Dhandhera), pseudo-agnation (Bundela-Dauwa), and dispensation (Bundela-Khangar).

In the phase of kingdom formation in Bundelkhand unilineal

descent was significant as the basis of group- formation, in the assignment of status and struggles for power. The primary identities of the ruling group and of its allies and adversaries were based on clanship rather than on caste as generally understood in north Indian ethnography. Among the three-kuri-Rajput of eastern Bundelkhand, clan exogamy combined with circulating connubium of the three clans provided the principle for inclusion and exclusion. As we shall see in the following chapter, along with the strong clanship and muted caste membership affiliation with, and legitimisation through, a sect—the Pranami Sampradaya—appears as an ancillary principle of Bundela kingship in the seventeenth century.

At a more general level, I have to reverse the hypothesis of sanskritisation to understand the dynamics of political processes in pre-industrial middle India as exemplified by the case at hand. Far from political power being converted into *jati* status to become legitimate and meaningful, the expansion of Bundela rule shows that under certain geo-political conditions throughout middle India, exclusion from a confirmed *jati* status was the means of gaining power and creating a new framework of statuses and offices.

Notes

1. Had each category comprised an equal number of clans, and the two categories as a whole been exhaustive for all Rajput clans of central India, we might have regarded the categories 'three-kuri' and 'thirty-six-kuri' as moieties. In the case at hand the clans comprising each category constitute distinct clusters, practicing 'territorial endogamy'. Moreover, there is a third category of intermarrying Rajput clans, the 'thirteen-kuri' (*terah kuri ke Rajput*), with a mixed territorial distribution, which I do not discuss here.
2. Kesava Das Misra, an eastern (*Sanadhya*) brahmin, was a noted Hindi poet. His family held the hereditary offices of royal mythographer (*pauranic*) and councillor in the court of the Bundela kings of Orchha. Maharaja Bir Singh Deva Bundela, the patron-king of Kesava Das, ruled at Orchha from circa 1606 to 1630. A junior son, Bir Singh Deva had usurped the kingdom of

Orchha from his elder brother under the protection of his ally and patron, the Moghul emperor Jahangir. Yet, as a native historian puts it, Bir Singh Deva was 'mindful of the sin he had committed...and feeling great remorse, in penitence made nine pilgrimages and offered innumerable sacrifices'. (Mazboot Singh translated by Silberrad op. cit.: 114.) Kesava Das officiated at the coronation ceremony one year before he composed the poetic biography, *Bir Singh Caritra.*

3. My inference that Pancham's exile was caused by a dispute over inheritance is supported by the following observations: (a) The partition of heritage amongst sons within the ruler's lifetime is known historically to have been a Bundela custom as indicated, for example, by Chhatrasal's letters regarding the partition of Panna heritage (cf. Gupta, 1958, pp. 151-3); (b) The phrase '*bala bahikrama*' (from Sanskrit, *bala vayahakrama*, meaning 'young age') in the text indicates Pancham was a minor at the time of his father's death. Although the Dharmasastra enjoined upon kings the duty of protecting the interests of minor heirs' (Kane 1946: iii, 574), the expropriation of Pancham's share by his brothers appears to signify weak royal authority in a pricipality (kingdom or domain) of that period. Because of insufficient evidence I am unable to pursue Professor Derrett's suggestion (in a personal communication) that Pancham was the son of a lady whose status was open to doubt.
4. Mahoni is recorded by the name Mau-Mahoni in Bundela chronicles. Mau (26°N.79'E.) is a village on the eastern bank of River Pahuj lies in Jalaun District while Mahoni itself lies a short distance across the river in Gwallior territory.
   Kundar (25°26'N, and 78°57'E.) is located in Tikamgarh District. Kateragarh is
   > 'better known as Katera, the seat of a Jagirdar and titular Raja in pargana Mau (Jhansi District) 26 miles S.-E. of Jhansi' (Silberrad, p. 105).
5. Elliot, basing himself on the testimony of a 'Mohammedan historian', advanced the 'racialist' view that the legend of the capture of Garhkundar is a Bundela myth fabricated to conceal the fact of their being the progeny of a Gaharwar Rajput from a Khangar concubine. In a similar vein, Tod constantly reduces the Rajput value of 'honour' in matters of bride-giving to a notion of racial purity. The fact of the matter is that giving away a woman was, for the royal clans, tantamount to capitulating territory. Purity of

blood, on the other hand, was preserved by preventing indiscriminate mixing, in the first place by the strict observances of patrilineal exogamy and the incest taboo.

6. This is a structural imperative because the series of hierarchically graded statuses cannot be extended either to the 'three-kuri Rajput' category amongst whose constituent clans there is non-hypergamous connubium or below it, where another opposition, that between the kshatriya (e.g. the 'three' and 'thirty-six-kuri' Rajput clans) and the non-kshatriya (e.g. the Khangar) becomes operative, leading to a qualitatively different basis for 'exclusion'.
7. Luard (1909:10), basing himself on the Khangar annals, mentions the names 'Bucha' for Khet Singh and 'Bhup Singh' for Hurmat Singh of Bundela chronicles whom Verma seems to have followed. According to Luard's sources, Bucha who was appointed governor at Garhkundar, had eight sons whom he assigned the eight forts of Tehrauli, Bamora, Kachra, Malhara, Chhoti-Parasin, Kanta-Kamta, and Sikri-Sunta. These sons were known as the *Ath garhiyaval* (Keepers of Eight Forts) a name which clung to their descendants. He also appends a list of twenty-nine Khangar clans (*gotra*), each identified with a place of domicile (*khairo*). The clans are totemistic and exogamous.
8. It is not possible to discuss the geo-political factors fully within the scope of this chapter. I allude to the over-all pattern in note 11.
9. Panwar sublineages intermarrying with the Bundela and the Dhandhera are descended from the four sons of Punyapal: from Ratansah, the Panwar of Karera; from Jetsah, the Panwar of Kairuwan; from Shankarsah, the Panwar of Barechha; from Chandrasena (the illegitimate son of a prostitute named Chandrabhaga), the Panwar of Ghati Mayapur.
10. The Panwar outside Bundelkhand are segmented into sub-castes. For the Waiganga valley see Russell and Hiralal 1916: iv: 340.
11. The regional political system never formed an effective part of a higher level power (cf. Cohn 1962:313-14, for levels of the political system in eighteenth-century India).
    Moreover, the ecological frontier for south-eastern expansion with ravines, forests, and plateaus was particularly favourable for swift guerrilla action by local battalions such as the Bundela commanded.
12. The east-west axis is a 'template', a standard unit of classification in areas of Rajput dominance. In its various applications, with of without accesory classifiers (e.g. elements of the terrain, viz. river,

plateau, valley, etc.) it may refer to indigenous regions and sub-regions. On account of its relative application, geographical or administrative areas cannot be fixed absolutely by means of this classifier. In this sense Fox's choice of the solar metaphor (minus the phosphorised Hallowe'en costumes) is appropriate for translating Rajput representations.

13. I have developed this theme in an unpublished paper, 'Rajput kinship and the social organisation of dominance in central India'.

CHAPTER II

Kingship, Territory and Property in Pre-British Bundelkhand

Each of the three basic terms forming the title of this chapter —kingship, territory and property—have suffered from neglect in the sociological and social anthropological analyses of Indian society. In the view of some scholars, the nature of the institution of kingship, as it might bear on an understanding of 'modern' Indian society and history, is recondite. Louis Dumont's attitude (1970:310) is representative of this class:

> As the royal function can hardly be observed nowadays, there is paucity of anthropological literature on this topic.... A picture of the whole would require that the extensive modern historical literature be brought into focus from a sociological point of view.

On the other hand, there is the attitude of anthropologists like F.G. Bailey who have, in opposition to Dumont's stress on ideology and ritual status in Indian society, brought into focus the changing institutional context of political behaviour. In his anthropological field studies in Orissa, Bailey imposes at the very outset, a typological grid contrasting the tribal system of the Kond with the caste system of the Warriors, even though an effort is made to discern interactions between the two systems in a political field within a changing arena dominated successively by (British) administration and political democracy (Bailey 1960). Like many analysts before and after him, Bailey holds an oversimplified picture of pre-administration rural socio-economic structure, emphasising the great gulf between the state and village as 'separate worlds' (Bailey, 1957:4). Interestingly enough, within his typological framework of tribe and caste he comes close to recognising that

> a part of Oriya political life must be seen as a segmentary system. In most Oriya villages in the Kondmals, the dominant caste are the Warriors. If we view all the villages as part of an interacting whole, then the links between the dominant landowning caste-groups in each village are segmentary: they resemble structurally the links between Kond clan territories. (Bailey 1961:13.)

However, as far as the overall political structure of the tributary states of Orissa is concerned, Bailey is unable to translate this formal resemblance into historical terms. As a first step, each Oriya state would provide the concrete locus for treating 'the villages as part of an interacting whole', and each state could be formally located in a segmentary structure of kingdom formation. But in this respect Bailey, like most students of the ethnohistory of pre-British India, works under a severe handicap. The only reports about these states and kingdoms in English were written by colonial officials. They made drastic summaries of a complex situation, which lacking language proficiency and scholarly motivation, they could not grasp fully. In the last chapter of his book *Caste and the Economic Frontier* (1957), Bailey grapples with the meagre information on pre-administration land-tenure in the tributary states of Orissa provided by Hunter and Macpherson, but is unable to decide whether or not sale of land was usual before 1855. As a social anthropologist he is interested in comparison, thus he observes:

> In Bisipara a system of land tenure probably similar to that of Zululand has fallen down before the play of market forces and legislative encouragement of private rights. (Ibid.: 244).

And in a footnote, he adds that 'the Raja was the spiritual head of Oriyas in the Kondmals' (Ibid.: 251). These are significant observations and we shall follow their implications in the analysis of data from the Bundelkhand region.

The colonial legacy of official reports on the working of indigenous political systems was to portray these polities as being in a state of anarchy. Indeed, these accounts would make it difficult to even speak of a system. Cohn (1962) and Shah (1964) provide much needed correctives to restore a sense of coherence in this area of study. It is relatively easy to see the reasons why Cohn does not explicate the nature of kingship in the Banaras region. When we first hear of the Raja of Banaras in the early eighteenth century, it is already in the context of what Cohn terms 'the secondary level' of the political system. This level refers to the emergence of successor states, such as Oudh and Bengal, following 'the dissolution of Moghal power, if not authority'. Mansa Ram, the father of the first Raja of Banaras, was a Bhumihar brahmin. He worked initially for the local *amil* (tax collector) in Jaunpur district and was later himself elevated to the office of *amil* at the court of Mir Rustam Ali, who administered the four districts of the Banaras province under Saadat Khan, Nawab Vazir of Oudh. Although Mansa Ram himself was one of four brothers whose father 'controlled' a few hundred *bighas* in a village in Jaunpur district, at the death of Saadat Khan in 1739, he (Mansa Ram) 'through lavish presents and the promise of paying to Safdar Jung (Saadat Khan's nephew and successor) an enhanced revenue, obtained a *sanad* (royal grant) for his son, Balwant Singh, which made the latter Raja of Banaras, Jaunpur and Mirzapur' (Cohn, 1962:314). The point is that in this particular situation, as contrasted with the case in Orissa (already discussed) and in Bundelkand (to be discussed), there was no inherent *descent-based* legitimacy for the Raja of Banaras. Rights to territory in these other instances were intrinsically related to descent. Cohn shows how the legitimacy of Chait Singh, Balwant Singh's successor, was brought into question by the Nawab of Oudh. It could be restored only through the intervention of Warren Hastings. Furthermore, the secondary level authority, the Nawab of Oudh, was progressively constrained to bestow legitimacy on successors of this upstart family because the Raja, howsoever reluctant to pay up the full revenue, could be made to yield something. This was more than would have been possible under chaotic conditions created by rebellious zamindars, were the Raja to be removed. It was, as Cohn aptly puts it, 'the balancing of relative weakness' in the face of a determined ground-swell of resistance from the local zamindars which provided the cement for the system. Finally, we should note that the rights to land and its produce—whether of the local- level zamindars or of the Raja—are discussed in this context as aspects of 'control'. This is connected with the fact that the majority of Raja-level ('regional level') controllers of land were, like the Raja himself, tax-farmers (Cohn, 1969:62) rather than *jagirdars* etc.; i.e., holders of 'estates of rights of administration' (Gluckman, 1965:42). In short, the particular regional circumstances of Banaras raj predispose the analyst (Cohn) to view the question of legitimacy in a political, rather than in a status, context just as it leads to emphasising 'land control' at the expense of multi-layered rights over land and its produce.

In order to improve upon the static implications of the 'little kingdom' and 'block' conceptualisations of political systems in pre-British north India, R.G. Fox (1971) has utilised a model of interaction between two major variables; unilineal descent-groups of the Rajputs and state-hinterland political relations in 'pre-industrial' North India. Each is treated as an independent variable; however, some ambiguity arises on account of his use of the term 'political' as an umbrella concept. The use of this concept to characterise the functions of a large number of intermediary beneficiaries between the producers and the State is fairly unexceptionable. In this respect Fox's formulation is a variation on Cohn's 'levels of political system'. However, the system of Rajput descent-groups at the regional and local levels demands finer scrutiny than afforded by discerning its political functions alone. This is not the place to go into an extended critique of Fox's notion of 'stratified lineages' which is a borrowing from Fried's interpretation (1957) of the political function of Chinese lineages. For a start, unless we assume the existence among the Rajputs of 'pre-industrial' North India, of the institution of warlordship which characterised Chinese society at a comparable historical phase, the comparison does not make sense. Secondly—and this is a more serious criticism—it is not possible to wish away the status dimension of caste and kingship for the study of institutionalised political behaviour among ruling groups. The manner in which Fox treats status as an aspect of ideology is unsatisfactory. If he were really serious about following the full implications of Dumont's approach to 'ideology', *Kin, Clan, Raja and Rule* would have been a very different kind of a book, incorporating, at least, a discussion on 'the royal function'. He speaks of 'an ideological model of genealogical descent which subsumed both local corporate kin bodies and dispersed tenuous status categories with little behaviour significance', and, after adducing a parallelism between this approach and Dumont's demonstration of a continuity of organising principles between caste and kin as in southern India, adds that, 'I note the emulation and duplication of an ideology of genealogical descent between local lineage and dispersed caste' (Fox 1971:23). Fox thereby substitutes extensionist psychology for a structuralist or a historical causal analysis. On the more substantive level, Tambiah (1973:79) has suggested the relevance of the rule of lineal, before collateral, heirs in the Hindu domestic sphere which ought to be matched against the corporateness of Rajput lineages. A significant 'status' contrast with Chinese society—the specification of a woman's right to property among Hindus—should alert us to the distinctive cultural significance of dowry, and of affinity in general. These dimensions are lacking in Fox's account.

Boundary Conditions

For at least three hundred years until its integration into the Indian union in 1948, the Bundelkhand region formed the territory of native states. On the basis of geo- political variation, it is possible to divide this region into four zones: (1) the cis-Jamuna Doab and the plateau tract. The British districts of Jhansi, Jalaun, Hamirpur and Banda lay in this zone. (2) The plateau and ravines between the Chambal and Betwa rivers. Among the Bundela kingdoms in this zone were Chanderi, Datia and Orchha. (3) The plateau and forest—from the river Betwa in the west, as far as the Bhanrar ranges of the Vindhyas in the east, and to the river Narmada in the south. The Bundela kingdoms of Bijawar, Panna, Ajaigarh and Charkhari, and the Panwar kingdom of Chhatarpur lay in this zone. Chhatarpur was founded by a Panwar Rajput retainer of Panna Raja in 1785 AD. The forest is most extensive to the east of river Ken. Panna, the capital of the Bundela kingdom of the same name, is located precisely in this forested and isolated tract. This zone which I designate as Eastern Bundelkhand, is indigenously subdivided and classified in a variety of ways. Any low-lying infertile tract, e.g. some of the land falling in the present *tehsils* of Chhatarpur and Rajnagar is known literally as 'inferior lowland' (*ghatiya khalen*). The area of river Dhasan is known as *dangahi* (from *dang*, meaning forest). The area traversed by the river Ken is designated Gudana (from Gond); its hilly parts are still inhabited by the Gonds, although their provenance today is not as extensive as it was in pre-Bundela times. A subdivison of Gudana is known as Khatola which seems to have been the name of a province of the medieval Gond kingdom. Today, this term is applied locally to a part of Malehra in the former state of Bijawar and to the dialect of Bundeli language spoken in parts of Chhatarpur and Bijawar. (4) The cis-Narmada southern zone. This zone shares many of the physical characterstics of zone 3 but the river valley plains of the Narmada are more fertile than those innundated by the river Ken. There is also a good proportion of black cotton soil in this region. From the late eighteenth century, this zone came under the direct administration of the Marathas and, later, of the British. In its political evolution, therefore, it is comparable to zone 1. The British districts of Sagar, Damoh and Jabalpur lay here.

In this discussion my focus will be on zone 3 during the 'pre-British' period. The term 'pre-British' does not have in these territories, the unequivocal sense it possesses for areas directly under British administration. A brief excursus into the history of

Bundelkhand from about 1734 AD onwards is called for. The maximum extent of Bundela territory under the hegemony of a single ruler was the kingdom of Panna carved out by Chhatrasal (1675 AD). Before his death in 1734 AD, Chhatrasal had bequeathed one third of his territory (Jhansi and Jalaun) to the Marathas, and the rest was divided amongst his heirs. Between the Treaty of Bessein in 1802, and the year 1886, almost all the Maratha share of his inheritance had passed under British control. This territory, known as British Bundelkhand in pre-Independence literature, was administered under the British district system and is of no direct concern to us here. However, at the same time (1802 AD) as the Maratha territories of Bundelkhand passed into British control, the Bundela territories also came under the purview of the British Political Officer who was attached to the forces operating in Bundelkhand with the purpose of introducing order into the civil administration. This appointment was formalised in 1811, when the country was settled, as Agent to the Governor General of India stationed at Banda (British Bundelkhand). In 1854 the Central India Agency was created in the interests of further rationalisation of political relations with the native states. This process continued throughout the twentieth century until the integration of these states into the Indian Union in 1948.

If we now work our way back into the history of this region it will be seen that before the establishment of British paramountcy in the eighteenth century, the indigenous political systems of Bundelkhand had been articulated with two centralised polities, the Maratha and the Moghul. Writing about the Banaras region, Bernard Cohn distinguishes four levels of political system in eighteenth century India—the Imperial (British or Moghul), the Secondary (the Nawabs of Oudh), the Regional (the Raja of Banaras) and the Local (Rajput lineages). In Bundelkhand, from the mid-eighteenth century to the third decade of the eighteenth century, it is possible to discern only two levels: the 'attenuated' Imperial (Moghul) and an osmosis between the regional and the local on account of the clan-based structure of indigenous polity. I shall return to the local-regional level in greater detail later, but a few characteristics of the kingdom-imperial relations during this phase may be noted.

Whether or not the kingdom of Orchha formed a part of Akbar's domain is contentious. Irfan Habib says that the *Ain-i-Akbari* ignores it. It is known however, that the Bundela chiefs of Orchha and Datia were under the suzerainity of Jahangir and the later Moghuls. Their status, however, was much more autonomous than that of *jagirdars* or even official *mansabdars* in the Daob. Their only obligation to the Emperor was the payment of tribute (*khiraj*). Military support was expected but was frequently given with much reluctance. For the sake of their autonomy, at once social and political, the Bundela chiefs, unlike certain other Rajput chiefs of Rajputana, never consented to send their daughters to the imperial harem. On the other hand, they participated in the Moghul wars of succession much to their own advantage, and as war-leaders in an inhospitable tract, little known to the Moghul outsiders. Throughout this early phase, the imperial administration had formally provided a secondary level through the offices or *Subahdars* and *Kiladars*. But the imperial officials were constantly under attack from local chiefs.

Only towards the close of the first phase, which corresponds with the death of Chhatrasal, did a secondary level proper, (equivalent to the Nawab of Oudh in Banaras) in the form of the Bangash Nawabs of Farrukhabad, appear on the Bundelkhand political scene. But its consolidation was delayed by the course of its initial failure. In 1729 AD the army of Muhammad Khan Bangash suffered a decisive defeat at Jaitpur (District Hamirpur, U.P.) from the joint forces of the Bundelas and the Marathas.

The available historical record of circumstances under which Chhatrasal obtained Maratha help in the battle of Jaitpur defies a cut and dried classification of Maratha authority in Bundelkhand into any one of the levels suggested by Cohn. The military administration of the Marathas was based on the principle of theocratic warfare. There is documentary evidence that the idiom of a military pact, between the Peshwa Bajirao and Chhatrasal Bundela, was that of common religion and 'kinship'. The kinship idiom recurs in the deed of inheritance by which Chhatrasal bequeathed one third of his territories to the Maratha Peshwa, and in letters exchanged between their successors. Even the Treaty of Alliance between Peshwa Bajirao and Hirdeshah, Chhatrasal's son and successor to the *gaddi* of Panna, is essentially similar to those commonly signed between two Bundela chiefs. Consequent upon their gaining a territorial foothold in Bundelkhand, the Marathas entered into similar Treaties of Alliance with other Bundela kingdoms of the area. Through the office of the Subahdar in Bundelkhand, the Maratha court at Pune established representative rule in the territories bequeathed to them by Chhatrasal. These were interspersed throughout Bundelkhand although most of them lay in zones 1 and 4. The transfer of territories from the successors of Chhatrasal to the Marathas in the remaining areas was by no means a smooth process. The Bundelas yielded territory in a piecemeal fashion, although political and military pressure was exerted by the Marathas to force their claim. The correspondence between the Peshwa and the sons of Chhatrasal—Hirdeshah, the Raja of Panna, and Jagatraj, the Raja of Jaitpur—acknowledges a sentiment of brotherhood. The Peshwa refers to Chhatrasal as '*Kakaju*' (father's younger brother); this is the term which Hirdeshah and Jagatraj used for their father. In proportion to his share of Chhatrasal's estate, the Peshwa agreed to pay a third of the cost of building the royal cenotaph (*chhatri*) for Chhatrasal, exactly as a real son would.

It was not until a war of succession for the *gaddi* of Panna broke out among the descendants of Hirdeshah that a secondary level proper became the main external arena in the political conflicts of local Bundela *rajas*. The complicated pattern of political alliances between local chiefs, and the Marathas on the one hand, and the Muslim Nawabs on the other, is the theme of the history of Bundelkhand for nearly twenty years following the death of Chhatrasal in 1731 AD. The entire Rajput-held area of Bundelkhand in zone 3 had, by this time, become fragmented into numerous petty chiefdoms. The grant of hereditary jagirs and offices to Bundela and non-Bundela incumbents, the majority of whom were held together by little more than their common sentiment of kinship to the Panna raj under Chhatrasal, was the first cause of this fragmentation. The second cause was the intrusion, again of kinship as an ancillary principle of legitimisation of authority at the secondary level of the political system, the Marathas and the Nawab of Banda. Finally, the political systems of eastern Bundelkhand were truly threatened at this time, not only by the disappearance of the nominal authority of an attenuated Imperial level but also because the secondary levels were, as just noted, vertically tied up with the local and regional levels through the fiction of kinship.

After the Treaty of Bassein between the Marathas and the British East India Company in 1802, the foundations of a political system, which was to last for the next one hundred and fifty years, were laid. The British dispensation in Bundelkhand rested on the military subjugation of the Marathas and the Nawab, and the legal restoration of a segmentary state structure among the Rajput chiefs. In the changed political and economic setting, what could no longer be achieved by kinship and custom was effected by legal provisions, especially by the paramount control of civil law pertaining to land ownership. The definition of social dominance was bound to have serious repurcussions on the structure of agrarian class relations.

Rights in Land and Status Framework: Bundelkhand zone 3

On the basis of genealogical and legendary information, backed by observations made in the course of fieldwork, I concluded in the previous chapter that the Bundelas' quest for territory for kingdom-formation was validated in a framework of unilineal descent. The evidence also suggested that the actual process of kingdom-formation was not characterised by an emulation of the standards of a higher caste-group but that 'under certain geo-political conditions throughout middle India, exclusion from a confirmed *jati* status was the means of gaining power and creating a new framework of statuses and offices'.

The dynastic and dominance levels of the Bundela genealogy,

like the legendary and mythical levels, form integral parts of a hierarchical series of encapsulated history. Using the genealogy as an aid to the study of the past at these levels, one finds legends legitimising the rule of the Bundela over territory. The intervention of a charismatic holy man, the occurance of a test of prowess for the king, and his disappearance rather than death are recurrent themes in foundation stories of Bundela kingdoms. It is strikingly obvious that here we have examples of legitimisation of royal authority by founders of sects rather than by brahmin priests. The Hindu kingdoms of Bundelkhand provide a context in which the brahmin's influence was not as strong as in those regions squarely under Muslim domination (Dumont 1970:155). Not surprisingly, the ritual hierarchy of castes is unable to yield the principle of legitimisation of power into authority in Bundela kingdoms. Nor is this true of Bundelkhand alone. Mayer mentions that in the territory of the former princely state of Dewas Senior in Malwa, Gokulashtami, the main ritual of the year, was, to borrow a tag from E.M. Foster, 'not priest-ridden but ruler-ridden' (Mayer 1958: 420).

It is true that modern scholarship has demolished the alleged mutual opposition between caste and sect as terms of sociological discourse. For instance, as a matter of empirical fact, Louis Dumont's thesis (Dumont 1960:33-60) that the caste system represents a model of society formed by 'man-in-the world', while sect refers to the influence of the renouncer, 'the individual-outside-the world', has been challenged (cf. Burghart 1983). There are enough continuities between the life and thought of renouncers and their imbrication in the world of castes (cf. Jain 1999: Chapter 5) Conversely, community-based holy men—*gurus* and *swamis* of all description—display degrees of social attachment that are markedly sectarian.

However, when one considers the process of legitimising temporal power in terms of a 'liturgy' (Hocart 1969)—castean or otherwise—there exists a strong correlation between, on the one hand, forested, rocky and secluded regions and, on the other, the dominance in such regions of sectarian and charismatic holy men, (rather than brahmins), who articulate and legitimise the rebellious and anti-establishment 'rule' by warriors and upstarts (cf. Ramachandra Guha 1994: Chapter 4). For instance, in the Bundelkhand milieu it is said that 'a *dakait* of yesterday becomes the *raja* today and vice versa'. It is obvious that the hegemony of divine kingship contains within itself, at lower *praja* levels, the seeds of its destruction. Here the isolated and protected geopolitical and ecological conditions favouring a direct and unmediated relationship between *raja* and *praja* favoured the rise of sectarian leaders as legitimisers of kingship. And the character of kingship itself was surcharged by *charisma* with magic and military prowess emanating not from the confirmed caste status of the protagonists but from what we may call extra-caste, if not the anti-caste, socio-cultural ambience of their power. The principal structural framework for this extra-caste order was provided by clanship, lineage and sectarian affiliation that enabled a conquered territory (the region) wider than the territory of descent-based rights alone (the locality) to fuse together into a kingdom (*rajya*). The 'kingdom' comprising the ruler and his 'territory-cum-people' (Dumont 1967) became charged with sacred cosmological properties.

On the more substantive aspects of land rights in zone 3, there is a paucity of historical data and, as yet, of search and systematic analysis of *pargana*-level records comparable to the work done by historians, for example, in eastern Rajasthan (cf. Chandra and Gupta 1996). In the absence of such research, however, I would like to offer two case studies from the kingdoms of Panna and Bijawar in Bundelkhand zone 3 to ask some anthropological questions of extant data and to make a few suggestions concerning the fruitfulness of a combined anthropological and historical attack on these questions. In this preliminary exploration, let us bear in mind the social, cultural and political features of 'pre-British' indigenous rule in this area already delineated: (1) descent-based rule; (2) procedures for the legitimisation of power into authority not subsumed by a 'caste' model; and (3) relatively loose political integration with centralised 'paramount' polities.

Maharaja Chhatrasal Bundela of Panna (1649 AD to 1731 AD)

Chhatrasal was the founder of the kingdom of Panna. His career is relatively well-documented (Gupta 1958; Singh 1973; 1975). From a sociological point of view, his career makes an interesting case for reconstructing the pattern of claims to rights in territory and the significance of kinship as a status factor in political transactions.

But first a summary of the historically documented aspects of his rise and career as the founder and consolidator of an independent Bundela kingdom. Chhatrasal's patrilineal ancestor in the sixth ascending generation belonged to a cadet-line of the ruling house of Orchha. A grant of the year 1612 AD enumerates the 13 villages by revenue units (*pargana*) and subunits (*mauja*) to whose income Chhatrasal's paternal grandfather was entitled in perpetuity. The income from this estate (*jagir*), is granted to the holder as remuneration for service and administration (*seva-sasan*). The grantee is referred to as 'brother' (*bhaiyya*). The tile of Chhatrasal's father, Champat Rai is Rao, a title given in Bundela kingdoms to holders of estates of rights of administration in the cadet lines. Champat Rai, like his forefathers, lived in Mahewa village (presently in Chhatarpur district). This village remained Chhatrasal's military capital throughout his life.

The contrast between Chhatrasal's earlier status as co-sharer of rights in *jagir* at Mahewa and his later status as the king of Panna is clearly brought out in an excerpt from a 'letter of reminiscence' which he wrote to his son Jagatraj in 1730 AD Chhatrasal recounts his meeting with a charismatic holy man (Prannath) who beckons him on to Panna. At that time Chhatrasal describes himself as a freebooter who engages in 'warfare for territory (*riyasat ko upaya*) for the sake of my children' and plunders 'to feed my soldiers'. Having subdued the Gond raja of Panna and found diamonds in the territory, Chhatrasal says to the sage, 'With your permission, your Holiness, I shall now return to Mau (Mau-Mahewa). I am not a king of anywhere, nor was my father a king nor will I be one'. Upon this Prannath says, 'You are destined to be the ruler of a kingdom. You will live for a little under a hundred years and see the face of your grandson'. Chhatrasal replies, 'Your Holiness, I do not have a son, what to say of grandsons and great grandsons'. Whereupon the sage replies, 'You will have sons the like of whom no one has, and you shall have illustrious descendants'. (In the year 1675 AD Maharaja Chhatrasal camped at Khejra in Panna and became the king of Panna.)

It is quite clear that Chhatrasal's quest for a kingdom (a territorial domain as contrasted with plunder) is motivated by a desire to establish a princely lineage and found a royal house. The phrase '*larkan ko lane riyasat ka upay karat houn*' (warfare for territory for the sake of my children) is a clear indication of this attitude. The question of male progeny (sons, grandsons, and great grandsons) is inextricably bound to the founding and perpetuation of a royal lineage. The right of a Bundela *jagirdar* to concerted effort (*udim*) for acquiring a kingdom is conceptualised as *bhum* (literally, land or territory). Literature dealing with this right in the former Rajputana states (present-day Rajasthan), has tended to define it in terms of a tenure by birth right (clanship) and to contrast it with tenures granted by the ruler (cf. Thorner 1956). According to Thorner (basing himself on Tod), the *bhum* tenure was highly coveted as the king could not interfere with it; indeed, the king, himself would crave for *bhum* rights in a few villages. Our data from pre-British Bundelkhand suggests a more dynamic interpretation of this 'right' or 'tenure'. It should be referred back to a time when the Rajput kingdoms were still proliferating by segmentation from the prior royal lineages; i.e., when a 'frontier' for expansion existed. In this context, the right of the *bhumia* (holders, both Rajput and non-Rajput) consisted not only in confirmed possession of the lineage territory but also (in the case of the Rajputs) in carrying out warfare, raid and plunder to extend their territorial possessions, with the purpose of establishing royal authority over them. The latter process was known as *bhumiawat* (cf. *Chhatraprakasa*: 12:100).[1]

Chhatrasala's policy of expansion and consolidation was two-pronged. On the one hand, he was related to the ruling Bundela houses of Orchha, Datia and Chanderi by ties of descent-based rule. As a descendant in one of the cadet lines of Orchha he held rights of jagirdar in Mau-Mahewa and cognate villages. The village of Mau-Mahewa in this domain remained his military capital, from where he carried out raids for acquiring territorial and other possessions to form a kingdom. The latter task was accomplished in 1875 AD with the capture of Panna. However, throughout his life he also engaged in predatory warfare against regional representatives of the central authority of the Moghuls. These campaigns conform to the narrow and technical notion of *bhumiawat*. The code of conduct between Bundela ruling houses forbade attacking each other's territory, but *bhumiawat* in other territories, especially those under the administrative and military control of alien chiefs (non-Bundela Rajputs and others), and appointees of the central government, was a matter of redeeming one's honour. Unless we take into account both the processes of consolidating the rule in Panna raj and carrying out raids in outlying territories, it is not possible to grasp the exact significance of the local saying related to the territorial limits of Chhatrasal's prowess:

It Jamuna ut Narmada, it Chambal ut Tons,
Chhatrasal so laran ki, rahi na kahu hons.

(From Jamuna in the north to Narmada in the south, from Chambal in the west to Tons in the east; no one [within these limits] has the courage to fight Chhatrasal.)

If we were to abide by a conception of 'stratified lineages' such as Richard Fox advocates for dominant Rajput groups in nineteenth century Uttar Pradesh, Chhatrasal should have been subordinate to the ruling houses of Orchha, Datia and Chanderi, belonging as he did, to a cadet lineage. To be sure, Chhatrasal starts his career in that position but gradually builds himself up as a *primus inter pares* with his 'brothers,' the rulers of Bundela kingdoms which preceded Panna. A treaty with Orchha, Datia and Chanderi kingdoms dated 25 April 1721, addresses

Chhatrasal as 'Maharaja' along with the two other Bundela rulers—those of Chanderi and Orchha. The ruler of Datia, on the other hand, belonging as he did to the Gujar caste, enjoys only the title of 'Rao'. Another indication of Chhatrasal's equality of status with rulers of other Bundela kingdoms is furnished by the fact that he relinquished the paternal *jagir* held from Orchha. In explaining the significance of this act, Chhatrasal writes in a letter addressed to the State officials of Panna, dated 11 November 1730:

> My honourable father, Rao Champatrai, was a jagir-holder in Orchha, and I desire it to be returned to them (those of Orchha; *Orchhewalan*). When I have obtained and won territory by my own prowess, why should I retain the name of a *jagir*-holder? Quite gladly should that *jagir* along with the instrument (*sanad*) be handed back to those of Orchha. Let there be no contention with them (about it) for the past or in the future. Since we descended from those of Orchha we have a right (*huq*), but we are not beholden to them for any favours...

A number of letters, written by Chhatrasal and to him, furnish a full picture of the manner in which he settled, within his lifetime, rights of administration over estates, among his principal sons, subsidiary sons, other relatives, and to those who served him in warfare. In this correspondence, the extent of territory included in the kingdom of Panna, is expressed in two ways; firstly, by the number of *parganas*. There were 40 *parganas* in the kingdom. They were smaller than the Moghul *mahals*. A second measure was according to the annual income received from the territory. By this reckoning the kingdom of Chhatrasal has been estimated to yield Rs. 1,53,000,000 per annum. While this represented the income from land revenue, the other sources of earning were the diamond mines of Panna, levying of *chouth*, and yield from plunder. The royal treasuries at Panna, Mahewa and Jaitpur are estimated to have held Rs. 5,000,0000. Besides this, there was separate amount of Rs. 8,00,00,000 whose existence was revealed by Chhatrasal to his son and successor Hirdeshah, shortly before his death. And all this treasure excluded the gold, silver, and ornaments obtained in plunder and deposited in the royal treasury.

Chhatrasal bequeathed the major share of his kingdom to his principal sons. The relative status of those sons (for four of these there is a historical record; Hirdeshah, Jagatraj, Padamsingh and Bharatichand) was determined not by order of birth, but by the status of their mothers as senior or junior queens of the ruler. Thus Hirdeshah, though younger than Padamsingh and Jagatraj, was nominated heir apparent (*pataut rajkumar*) to the seat of Panna because his mother, Devkunwar, of the Panwar clan was Chhatrasal's senior queen (*patrani*). Besides Panna, he was also granted Kalinjar and Shahgarh. His territories yielded an annual revenue of Rs. 38 lakhs. The male issue of Chhatrasal's second queen—Dankunwar of Dhandhera clan—was Jagatraj. Jagatraj's mother, on grounds of his seniority in age over Hirdeshah, made every effort to obtain his succession to the throne of Panna. But she could not persuade Chhatrasal to flout Bundela custom. Jagatraj had to rest content with territories in Jaitpur, Ajaigarh and Charkhari, which yielded an annual revenue of Rs. 33 lakhs. As to his eldest son, Padamsingh, also born of a junior queen, Chhatrasal had as early as 1689 AD, granted him the *pargana* of Jigni, the seat (*baithak*) of Jigni town, the title 'Rao', and royal paraphernalia consisting of jewellery, caparisoned elephants, carpets etc. The estate yielded an annual revenue of Rs. 3.5 lakhs. A fourth son, Bharatichand was similarly given a share in the kingdom worth Rs. 2 lakhs per annum, within Chhatrasal's lifetime (letter No. 4, 1669). Besides granting estates of rights in administration to his principal sons, Chhatrasal granted two *parganas* (Jalalpur and Darsinda) with an annual income of Rs. 6 lakhs, to his daughter- in-law (wife of Jagatraj), Jaikunwar, for her bravery in the battlefield against Mohammed Khan Bangash (letter No. 37, 1726).

The dispensation listed above would account for a little more than half of the total estates claimed to be under Chhatrasal's possession. Although he had promised to hand over a third of his kingdom to the Maratha Peshwa Baji Rao, he did not alienate any of his estates to the Peshwa within his lifetime. In fact, in a letter to Hirdeshah (letter No. 39), Chhatrasal confided to his heir apparent that the Peshwa had been told that his (Chhatrasal's) kingdom was worth Rs. 1 crore only. In the same letter, Hirdeshah was advised not to part with the promised share to the Peshwa but try and meet his demand with money payment only. Chhatrasal's sons and other relatives were known as *jagirdars*, while those who were holders of service tenures were known as *maimardars*. Besides these estate-holders, who were bound to the ruler by set duties, there were holders of *muafi* and *padaragh* i.e. recipients of benefices in religious charities who were not called upon to perform martial duties for the ruler. The *jagirdars*, by and large the ruler's relatives, had to provide only a specific number of infantry and cavalry when commanded to do so; the *maimardars* had to pay, in addition, an annual quit-rent. This was one sign of their inferior status vis-a-vis the *jagirdars*. It seems that the *jagirdars* themselves constituted a hierarchy. The ruler's principal sons enjoyed a highly privileged status; as we have seen in Chhatrasal's own lifetime, Hirdeshah and Jagatraj operated very much as rulers of Panna and Jaitpur respectively. Chhatrasal preferred to stay in his military capital, Mau-Mahewa. However, a built-in check to the ambition and expansionist designs of the sons, was insured since relatives and non-relatives of the rulers were simultaneously *jagirdars* and *sardars*. The latter term refers to office-holders in the state bureaucratic machinery. It should not be forgotten that the territories made over into estates of rights of administration to the various categories of sons, other relatives, *maimars* and *sardars* precluded those that were administered directly by the ruler. They were known by the Moghul term *khalsa*.

In so far as the above estates of rights of administration were allocated, by and large, on the basis of kinship and recognition of services in warfare, a generalised sentiment of 'brotherhood' formed the 'moral and tactical' (Bloch 1971) bonds uniting the holder to the ruler, and to one another, within a regional political system. These rights were hereditary and upto the *pargana* level each territorial block was subject to a series of retreating or reversionary rights from the holder upto the king.

However, this analogy with property rights in Zululand breaks down at the village level. Looked at from the point of view of the kingdom polity, a village as a whole formed an estate of production. Our data for the village-level in pre-British Bundelkhand is very scanty. The answer to the question, 'Who were the holders of the estate of production?' is, therefore, both variable and difficult. The first point to note in this connection is that Chhatrasal, as the king of Panna, had dealings with at least two categories of landholders. Firstly there are those *patels* (headmen), *zamindars*, *tehsildars*, *amirs*, and *subahdars* who control land revenue in territories which comprise Chhatrasal's area of raiding rather than direct rule. As noted earlier, this area is covered par excellence by what may be called Chhatrasal's campaign of *bhumiawat*. The various title-holders and officials included in this category owe their allegiance to the imperial power; the Bundela *bhumiawati* is able to secure not only a booty but is also able to assert his political authority over and above the heads of imperial appointees. Failure to comply with the demand for *chouth* brought retribution—wanton pillage and the destruction of standing crops. These were acts which would, at one stroke instil terror in the hearts of the holders of estates of production and, also hit the imperial authority in its most sensitive spot, namely, its revenue-base. *Chhatraprakasa*, the poetic biography of Chhatrasal, is full of instances where such tactics were pursued. As noted earlier, there is nothing shameful about this campaign since, as *bhumiawat*, this was a legitimate form of rebellion. The latter are the creation of the imperial authority, and what the Bundela ruler of Panna does is only cut a share for himself from the estates of production. This is done by pressurising the holders of such estates in territories under imperial control.

There were, on the other hand, estates of production directly under the rule of Chhatrasal. These were administered either through his own officials (*khalsa*) or through holders of estates of rights of administration (*jagir*, *muafi*, *padaragh*, *maimar* etc.) or corporate bodies of kinsmen claiming ownership (*malikana*) of one or several villages. The latter could belong to any caste, and would be known either as *bhumiya* or *zamindar*. They would lease their lands to tenants, or have them cultivated by agricultural labourers. They would cultivate some of the lands with their own family labour, or adopt a combination of any of these possibilities. In any case, a distinction seems to have existed between these village-level holders of estates of production and their super-ordinates—the holders of estates of rights of administration. The latter lived in forts and towns, the former in villages. More importantly, from the latter's point of view, the gradations of agrarian statuses (landlord, tenant, sub-tenant etc.) within the village were subsumed by the important fact that the village was the unit on which devolved the obligation of paying up the revenue—either through the title of the headman or through representatives of zamindars or bhumiyas. This remained true even when land came into the market (cf. *bhej-barar* tenure in Banda district). It is in this precise sense that we may understand both the relationship and the separation of the 'two worlds' of the state and the village.

Bundela Thakurs of Bhagwan, Bijawar State

The founder of the kingdom of Bijawar was Bir Singh, a grandson of Chhatrasal, being the third son of Jagatraj of Jaitpur. Jagatraj's eldest son, Kirat Singh, had predeceased his father, leaving behind two sons, Guman Singh and Khuman Singh. There was a protracted conflict between Jagat Raj's grandsons (Guman Singh and Khuman Singh) and his second and third sons (Pahar Singh and Bir Singh respectively) for the kingdom of Jaitpur. For a time, brothers combined against brothers and those of ascendant generation were successful against those of descendant generation. However, after establishing himself as ruler of Jaitpur, Pahar Singh grew suspicious of Bir Singh. (The two were born of different mothers.) Along with his mother, and sister's husband (Anirudh Singh), Bir Singh fled from Jaitpur and retired to Brindaban, where his mother built a temple and eventually died. Shortly before his death, Pahar Singh came to terms with his nephews, Guman Singh and Khuman Singh. In

1765 AD he is reported to have bequeathed the kingdom of Jaitpur (with an annual income of Rs. 13,50,000) to his son Gaj Singh, assigned Chakiband (worth Rs. 1,62,000 per annum) to Khuman Singh, and Ajaigarh and Banda (worth Rs. 9,25,000 per annum) to Guman Singh. Following the reconciliation, Guman Singh invited his uncle Bir Singh to return and offered him a jagir near Mawai worth Rs. 80,000 per annum. Bir Singh asked for more, and in 1769 AD was granted additionally, the distant *pargana* of Bijawar. This provided Bir Singh with a base for expansion from where, with the help of his brothers,[2] he carved out the kingdom of Bijawar. Soon after his accession to the kingship of Bijawar, Bir Singh, in customary Bundela fashion, assigned estates of rights of administration to all three of his brothers, and to one brother-in law. Thus his brothers Hate Singh, Arjun Singh and Khalak Singh became the founders of the patrilineages of Bhagwan, Silon, and Kupia Thakurs respectively, while his brother-in-law Anirudh Singh founded the Barethi family. The jagir of each of these relatives seems to have been worth Rs. 12,000 per annum.

We shall follow the vicissitudes of the patrilineage of Bhagwan Thakurs. The estate held by it shows inter alia an interesting transformation from being a jagir to becoming a zamindari. Unlike many other Bundela Thakur families, holding estates of rights of administration in villages, the Thakurs of Bhagwan are at once more numerous and reside in the various wards of the village Bhagwan itself. As the ex-ruler of Bijawar put it to me in a personal conversation, the special circumstances in Bhagwan are due to 'demographic lottery.' However, a historical analysis enables a discussion on the social and ecological factors that have affected the status and rights of the Bundela Thakurs of Bhagwan. There is incontrovertible evidence that in the mid and late eighteenth century, when the family of Hate Singh moved to live in a newly constructed fortress in the village, the Lodha cultivators were the zamindars of Bhagwan. The Bundela seem to have subdued them with the use of arms. During their phase of settlement in the village, the Bundela would have exercised only their superordinate administrative authority without disturbing Lodhas claims to estates of production. This was the phase when Bhagwan was, for the Bundela holders—the descendants of Hate Singh—properly speaking an estate of rights of administration, a jagir. Let us also note in passing that, unlike many other patrilineages holding jagirs in earlier Bundela kingdoms, those of Bhagwan did not have a frontier to expand. They were hemmed in by jagirs on all sides and thus constrained to retain and consolidate authority over territories initially granted to them by the Bijawar ruler. Vis-a-vis the royal seat at Bijawar, itself marked by weak centralisation, and operating as a confederation of agnatic and affinal lineages, the local patrilineal descent groups at Bhagwan would have presented a united front. There is evidence to support these propositions. We may rephrase the dynamic as follows: during the phase of jagir proper the Thakur holders of estate of rights of administration in Bhagwan looked to the royal seat at Bijawar as their house (*ghar*), and defined their status in the kingdom as co-sharers (*hissedar*) rather than as mere right-holders (*huqdar*). As proof of their status as co-sharers, they adduce the erstwhile custom (*quaida*), of reciprocal prestations between themselves and the royal household on the occasion of births, marriages, deaths etc. In general, the less the centralisation of power and authority in the kingdom, the more pronounced was the character of the kingdom-polity as a confederation of agnatically and affinally related patrilineages.

From the beginning of the nineteenth century there appears a pattern of factionalism between the constituent sublineages of Bundela agnates in Bhagwan, in which their corporate affiliation with the ruling house of Bijawar is a source of division rather than unity. The precipitating causes of conflict are both internal and external. During the reign of Ratan Singh of Bijawar (1810-1832 AD) the descendant of Hate Singh, the founder of the Bhagwan patrilineage, was Mohan Singh. Mohan Singh divided the jagir of Bhagwan into seven portions—six for his sons and one for himself. Each son got a *patti* of the village lands: thus the eldest, Daulat Singh, got Bazar *patti* and Bann; Jawahar Singh got Manikhera; Parichhat got Hardaul *patti*; Manakju got

Phutwari *patti*; and Mohan Singh retained for himself Sarkana. Although each son got an estate of income and administration, the rule of lineal primogeniture was adhered to. Thus the eldest son Daulat Singh, was known by the title Sawai Diwan (Sawai means 1¼), and was given the Bann (forest) as his extra share (*sawaya*). The other sons, as *jagirdars*, were entitled simply as Diwans.

The division of the *jagir* into *pattis* had important consequences. The patrilineages of Hate Singh fissioned off into six sublineages, and in each the share of *jagir* followed what may be termed as 'demographic lottery.' Also, after the death of Mohan Singh, conflict arose between the six brothers over the income from Sarkana (Mohan Singh's own estate). While four of the brothers were born of one mother, Bakhat Singh and Parbat Singh were born of another. Mohan Singh had predeceased the birth of Parbat Singh and had designated a *patti* for the son-to-be after a dream (thus the name of Parbat Singh's *patti* as '*Saphan*' meaning 'dream'). In his later years, Mohan Singh had lived with his youngest son, Bakhat Singh, who as the favourite son, claimed all the income from Sarkana after his father's death. This was unacceptable to the other sons and lead to an armed conflict between Bakhat Singh on one side, and the rest of the brothers on the other. The Bijawar ruler intervened and effected a settlement. Earlier the six brothers had to pay homage (*barbast* and *zabta*) to the Bijawar ruler by jointly providing 24 infantrymen, one elephant and one horse. This was commuted into money-income from the Sarkana estate which was confiscated by the State.

Although a settlement was thus effected on paper, it did not mark an end to hostilities between the State and the *jagirdars*. Fresh problems arose over the dispensation of Sarkana. Despite internal squabbles between the agnates, amongst whom the *jagirdari* of Bhagwan was shared, there remained a residue of 'jointness' which impelled the Bhagwan Thakurs to challenge any interference from the State. The descendants in Daulat Singh's sublineage continued to assert their dominant status as holders of *sawaya* rights and representatives of the Bhagwan *jagirdars* as a whole. Thus, Daulat Singh's eldest son, Kishor Singh, petitioned the Political Agent at Nowgong:

> Mauza Sarkana remained under our control for twenty years when we maintained an elephant, performed the last rites of my father and gave away my sisters in marriage. I did not get a share in my father's wealth. In lieu of all this I got income from Mauza Sarkana. The Durbar's order that I provide a *zabta* of 9 infantry and one horse is completely uncalled for. None of my ancestors ever maintained it. Similarly, the order to pay *barbast* is uncalled for. I never paid *barbast* in all my life... For twenty years following my father's death, Mauza Sarkana was under Bakhat Singh's control. As I did not receive any share in the income of that mauza for those many years, I am entitled to claim it...

Besides the non-payment of *barbast* and non-maintenance of *zabta*, the escheat of jagir lands (*patti*) due to the absence of male heirs was another basis on which the State appointed its own officials for collecting taxes in Bhagwan. This had the predictable consequence of skirmishes between State officials and local *jagirdars*, leading to double extortion from actual cultivators.

We begin now to understand the ideology of a kin-feudated polity. We begin to recognise that the typological contrast presented by Thorner between a 'tribal organisation' and a 'feudal' polity does not apply to the indigenous political systems based on kinship in pre-British India. One may indeed go further, and argue that considerations of kinship reappear tenaciously even though inter-kingdom relations during the nineteenth century are, on the whole, regulated by active interference on behalf of the paramount power by the British Political Agent.

An apt illustration is the case of the estate of Bakhat Singh's widow, referred to in the records as, Jamuniawali Kaki. (Kaki is the kinship term for father's brother's wife.) After Bakhat Singh's sole surviving male heir, Govind Singh, died, the Bijawar darbar decreed that the estate should continue in the possession of his widow during her lifetime. The sons of Bakhat Singh's four brothers claimed that, after her death, the *patti* would be equally divided among the heirs of the remaining four brothers. This latter promise does not seem to have been fulfilled, however. During the lifetime of Bakhat Singh's widow, the *jagir* of Saphan *patti* was confiscated by the Bijawar durbar—'on account of her disobedience.' The Jamuniawali kaki was sister to the Rao of Simariya, an affinal *jagirdar* of Panna durbar. Her lands (Saphan *patti*) lay on the border of Bhagwan (Bijawar State) and Simariya (Panna State). After Govind Singh's death, the Rao of Simariya tried to amalgamate his sister's estate with his own, which transformed the issue into a boundary dispute between Bijawar and Panna. The parties to the dispute were Bakhat Singh's collaterals and the Bijawar darbar on the one hand, and the Rao of Simariya and the Panna Darbar, on the other. Since this was an inter-state dispute, the British Political Agent appointed a Boundary Settlement officer to investigate it. In this officer's reports dated 18.12.1892 and 26.12.1892, there is clear affirmation of 'forcible aggression by Simariya' on the ground in the possession of Jamuniawali Thakurin. It is also reported that

> No fewer than 18 distinct orders… have been issued to Panna between April 14, 1882 and February 10, 1891, that the produce from the ground should be put in deposit until the case should be decided. On the 21st June 1883 Panna gave as a reason for not putting this produce in deposit that the claims had not yet been shown. Both Durbars were ordered to send in descriptions of their claims on the 14th October, 1882 and Bijawar's claims were shown to the Muzkuri and a description of it in answer to the *Diaikkar* given to him the same month. This was subsequently (15.5.1883) filed in the B.S.O.but notwithstanding repeated instructions Panna has neither sent in the description called for nor paid any heed to the orders to which I have above reported… (there) is conclusive proof that the ground in dispute was in possession of Bijawar from 1829 to the commencement of the dispute by 1882, and the value of its produce which should have been accumulated in deposit since that date should now be credited to Bijawar.

It is clear that a decision in favour of Bijawar durbar was taken above the heads of Bhagwan thakurs. With the confiscation of the jagir by Bijawar durbar, the local thakurs were left high and dry. It is small wonder that they continued to air their grievances in terms of kinship rights, but it is equally apparent that with the intervention of the paramount authority, these rights were set aside in favour of what was deemed, first and foremost, as inter-state relations. The Political Agents decisive comment on the petitions by the local thakurs reveals this quite clearly. In a judgement written on 13.4.1908 he says:

> The behaviour of these jagirdars has been unsatisfactory. I see no reason to support them against the Durbar. The Maharaja has full power in such matters as long as he is acting in good faith, as I have no doubt he is.

The last word in an issue like this should perhaps still rest with the thakurs. As the Bundelas of Bhagwan put it to me, 'The British separated the royal seat (*gaddi*) from the jagir.' This observation also epitomises the transition which took place from the pre-British to the British period in respect of kingship, territory and property in Bundelkhand.

Notes

1. Sleeman contributes a chapter on *bhumiawat* in his book; but his interpretation is vitiated by the 'premise of paramountcy,' which I have discussed elsewhere (Jain 1971). What we may salvage from Sleeman's account is the characterisation of *bhumiawat* as a kind of 'legitimate rebellion'.
2. Jagatraj is said to have 17 sons (Tiwari 1993:237).

CHAPTER III

Social Structure and Polity in Pre-British Bundelkhand: Notes on the House of Panna

Two aspects of pre-British Bundelkhand politics, already touched upon in the last chapter are, (a) the supralocal articulations of local and regional polities, and (b) the notion of magico-religious kingship vis-a-vis the secularised power of Bundelkhand chiefs and rajas. As a prelude to further notes on the house of Panna in pre-British Bundelkhand, we need to consider both these dimensions of power and status as depicted in recent literature. Perhaps the staunchest advocate of the Bundelas and their Rajput allies (Panwar and Dhandhera) being in the military service of the Moghals as '*naukars*' (servants), is Dirk H.A. Kolff (1990:120-51). He treats the Bundela as a 'spurious' Rajput clan whose adventurer-rulers sought legitimacy for their kingship through recognition by the Moghul rulers. The most outstanding example of this was Maharaja Bir Singh Deo Bundela of Orchha (1606-1630 AD) who ingratiated himself with the Moghal emperor, Jahangir. Kolff speaks of the Bundela rulers of Orchha merging into a natural service ideal, 'the service of Vishnu and that of the Moghal *badshah*' (ibid.: 122). The author's argument is that Bundela rajas and chiefs were military entrepreneurs for the Moghals besides being territorial lords. Kolff's book, subtitled, 'Ethnohistory of the

Military Labour Market in Hindustan, 1450-1750' covers three hundred years of military history in 199 pages. This is possible because Kolff finds a common factor 'contributing to the formation and upholding of the state' namely, the existence of a large military labour market constituted by peasant soldiers who moved from one region to another in search of employment. The success of each medieval state was, according to Kolff, ultimately dependent on how best it was able to command that market through its distribution of wealth. That this argument is extravagantly simplistic (cf. Roy 1994:28) is not our main point. Our main criticism is that it leads to the complete undermining of the primary and dominant identity of Bundela rulers as *yuvaraja* (princes) rather than highly fickle *mansabdars* (fief-holding subordinates) of the Moghals—a dichotomous duality that Kolff himself introduces. And this leads us straight to the second dimension, viz., the cosmogony of locally rooted magico-religious kingship in pre-British Bundelkhand. In this respect the anthropological literature on divine kingship (Evans-Pritchard 1962, Hocart [1936] 1970 and Feeley-Harnik 1985), is specially instructive and has a bearing on the nature and extent of secularisation or otherwise, of traditional Indian (Hindu) kingship (cf. Dumont 1962 and 1964). Based on his research in Garhwal and Kumaon, Guha (1994) has disputed the views of Dumont and R. Thapar about the secularisation of Indian kingship. However, as Madan (1999: 180-88) has cogently demonstrated,

> ...the relative autonomy that Dumont grants to the political function seems to be severely circumscribed more than might at first seem manifest. He is quite right, therefore, to express the relationship of spiritual authority and temporal power in terms of superiority and inferiority, or encompassing and encompassed, and not complete separation a'la Weber, who presented Hindu kingship as self-sufficient and fully secular.

The entailment of Hindu kingship with magico-religious beliefs and values in Bundelkhand will become manifest in what follows.

Political Systems in Pre-British Bundela Principalities: The Local and Regional Levels

The Oxford English Dictionary defines 'dominant' as 'ruling, prevailing, most influential; (of height) outstanding, overlooking others'. In explicating the principles of 'rule' in the old Bundela principalities, (Orchha, Datia, Chanderi, Panna, Bijawar and Ajaigarh), the point of departure must surely be 'territory-cum-people' (cf. Dumont 1964; Frykenberg et. al 1969) ruled over by a dominant group. In outlining the structural features of the dominant group and the dominated territory-cum-people, our selection of the right concepts from the analytical vocabulary of social anthropology is of utmost importance. Let us first of all reach a conclusion on the relevant features of the group 'Bundela', before attempting to relate it to the domain known as Bundelkhand.

Processes of Reproduction and Production

In the dominant groups, the principle of clanship regulated succession to the *gaddi*, the devolution of rights (*huq*) to territory and its produce, and the recruitment of women to ensure the continuance of the ruling 'line'. Besides the genealogical process of clan segmentation ensured by the last named function of the unilineal descent group, the specifically political process of socio-economic stratification was based on the regional social system of affinity and kinship, the economic system of production, and the imperatives of warfare.

Clanship, Affinity and Pseudo-kinship among the Bundelas

The Bundela clan is a patrilineal segment of the Rajputs (from Sanskrit *Raja putra*, the class of kingly sons). Throughout Bundelkhand, the Rajput class is subdivided into many kinds (*kuri*) and grouped into intermarrying patrilineal segments or clans. Bundelkhandi Rajputs are of the three kinds (*tin kuri ke Rajput*), viz., the Bundela, the Dhandhera and the Panwar. West of Bundelkand in Malwa, are the Rajputs of the thirty six kinds (*chhattis kuri ke Rajput*). Another grouping of Rajput segments also found in Bundelkhand is known as the Rajputs of the thirteen kinds (*terah kuri ke Rajput*).

A second meaning of the term *kuri*, when it refers not to the Rajput class as a whole or a grouping thereof, but to any single clan within a grouping (e.g., the Bundela segment among the three) is that of a patriline (*vamsa*). Genealogically it is possible to connect any one patriline with any other within the Bundela clan; thus in genealogical terms, a patriline is a branch of the clan. The difference between the two is that whereas the apical ancestor of a patriline is always a historical person, that of the clan at any particular level of segmentation, is a traditional character (a semi-historical personage of mythical origin). The higher up one moves in the clan genealogy, the greater is the mythological bias as opposed to the historical. The common feature in the collective representation of both the patriline and the clan is connected with the third meaning of the term, *kuri* (from the Sanskrit *ankura* meaning, 'a sprout', 'shoot', 'blade', 'a hair', 'water', 'blood': derivation in Hindi *kuri* meaning, n. 'a subdivision', 'a part', 'a portion': derivation in Desaja, *kuri* meaning 'plough'). A graphic representation of both the patriline and the clan in the metaphor of engendering and rearing is the traditional transcription of Bundela genealogy in the form of a creeper or a plant, with only the male descendants being shown as leaves on several branches. The following homology was explicitly stated to me by the Bundela informants of Bhagwan village in the Bijawar tahsil of Chhatarpur district, Madhya Pradesh:

blood : milk : : seed : water

I am tempted to argue, given the former milk-brotherhood relationship between the local Dauwa (cattle keepers) and the Bundela rulers (see below), and the present-day phrasing of marriage rules in terms of '*dudha bachana*', ('keeping the milk apart', or separation of marriage from the line of milk), that the female principle on the blood/milk side of the equation, and the male principle of land on the seed/water side, are unstated terms of the homology. The discovery of such a series is of considerable interest for the resolution of the problem of incest in a three-clan system of circulating connubium without a rule of marriage prescription in the Bundelkhandi Rajput grouping. Extolling the virtuous kingship of a seventeenth century Bundela ruler, Virasinghdeva of Orchha, a contemporary poet wrote:

Bali boi kirat lata, Karan kari do pat
Sinchi Vrsnghdeva ne, jab dekhi kumhalat.

Bali [the mythical king] sowed the creeper of Fame. Karan [the epical hero] it caused to sprout two leaves. When he saw it wilt, Vrsinghdeva [the Bundela king] watered it. The apical ancestor in this genealogical rendering is a mythical figure. His penultimate descendent is an epical hero who is followed by a historical king, the one in whose praise the couplet has been composed.

Recruitment: Affinity

Let us now examine, in turn, the three functions of the patrilineal clan mentioned earlier. The principle of clanship among the Bundelas is thrown into bold relief by their strict exogamic rule. There is an injunction against intra-clan marriage, and its violation is tantamount to incest. There is no positive prescription, but a highly marked preference for inter-clan marriage among the Rajputs of the three *kuri.* Indeed, the circulating connubium among the Bundela, Dhandhera and Panwar through a free and equal (non-hypergamous) exchange of women, has been realised to a very large extent in practice. The three clans—Bundela, Dhandhera and Panwar—are nominally assigned the gotras Kashyap, Vatsa and Vasista respectively, but the determination of prohibited degrees through the operation of what Karve has called 'the four-clan rule' (Karve 1968: 117-25) is of no avail in the Bundelkhandi Rajput grouping. The statement of the first rule of prohibited degrees is in terms of *dudh bachana* (keeping the milk apart or prohibition on an 'individual marriage with a person of the line of milk'), i.e., an ideological resistance to accepting a bride from the localised patriline (*khandan*) of one's mother (cf. Dumont 1964). Secondly, there is the familiar north Indian resistance to reversal in the direction of marriage expressed in the formula '*pao puj ke khandan se larki nahin li jaegi*' (Dumont 1964). However, in the long run, both these rules are honoured more in their breach amongst the three kinds of Bundelkhandi Rajputs, precisely on account of their being contradicted by a preference for intermarriage amongst the three clans. Through numerous examples, my Bundela informants were able to show how, with the exception of one or two marriages, or after a generation or two, (the formula is applied *ghum phirke*, i.e., in a roundabout way) marriages begin to be contracted in violation of the prohibitions (*bhai bahin ki sadi hone lagi*).

Thus we find that in terms of marriage rules and practice, the limits of endogamy in the Bundelkhandi Rajput grouping become so contracted as to arrive dangerously close to the point of incest. Political considerations in the ruling patrilines of the Bundelas had, in the course of their consolidating their rule (*rajya*) in Bundelkhand, made repeated intermarriages between the same houses a practical necessity. At the same time, in the wider Hindu ideology of their milieu, specifically that bearing on the conception of kingship, the offspring of such unions could easily be regarded as profane in terms of assuming the exalted status of dominance over 'territory-cum-people'. The dilemma was resolved through a ritual substitution of the mother's milk by that of the wife of a Ahir who thus became the *dai-ma* (foster mother and the mother of the portion) or *dudh-ma* (milk mother) for the princes and princesses. Her sons became *dudh-bhai* (milk-brothers) and her husband *dau* (father's elder brother) for the Raja's children. These service rights devolved patrilineally in particular Ahir lineages. On account of their special relationship with the Bundelas, these particular lines cut off marital relations with other Ahir patrilineages, and formed the Dauwa section of the Yadava clan.[1]

The Bundela-Dauwa league through the recognition of a surrogate milk-line has already alerted us to the potentiality of pseudo-kinship as an ancillary to the principle of clanship in the Bundelkhandi Rajput grouping. One solution to the problem of separating the narrow limits of endogamy from incest having been explained, we now consider how, in this system of clanship, the widest limits of exogamy were defined. Here again, the solution adopted is a typical one. The classification of their marital unions and its offspring, from the point of view of the males of any dominant patriline in the Bundelkhandi Rajput grouping, seems to have been a universal custom in pre-British Bundelkhand.[2]

At this stage, a digression into the customary mode of succession and inheritance among the Bundela, is in order. Bundela Rajputs married polygynously. The status of the *patrani* (the chief queen) in Bundela principalities is clear. She was the principal wife. The first male offspring (*narina santana*) of her womb (*garbha*), from the *auras* (breast, semen) of the ruler, would be the heir apparent (*pataut rajkumar*). In other words, she was the senior-queen, the mother of the senior son in the ruling line. The brothers (from the same womb) and half-brothers (from different wombs but the same *auras*) of the *pataut rajkumar*, were entitled to shares in the patrimony. However, a distinction was made between succession to the *rajya* and the inheritance of patrimony. The latter, having been declared profane by the author of *Vira Mitrodaya*,[3] all the *auras* sons were entitled to a share. Kingship (*rajya*) on the other hand, was held to be sacred; accordingly, a certain class of *auras* sons was excluded from the line of succession. It would seem that the basis of distinguishing sons who were excluded from the line of succession, from those included in it, was whether or not their mother was from a Rajput clan. It is important to note, therefore, that filiation from a new Rajput mother did not exclude them from establishing a Rajput house of their own. Thus, from the point of view of the males in the dominant line, there was a principal wife (usually a wife from within the Bundelkhandi Rajput grouping), junior wives (Rajput women) and subsidiary wives (non-Rajput women), begetters, respectively, of the heir apparent; junior sons included in the line of succession and patrimony; and secondary sons, excluded from succession, but included in patrimony.

Sons and Daughters

This statement provides a model of customary rules regulating succession, inheritance and marriage in a Bundela principality. From the viewpoint of our interest in exploring the limits of exogamy in the Bundelkhandi Rajput grouping, this model should be tested against historically known cases. The unions of Raja Chhatrasal, the Bundela military hero, and founder of Panna *rajya*, furnish a good, though extreme example, of the variety of unions and the kinds of sons that could be produced in a Bundela principality. He is mentioned as having married between 13 and 19 wives, from whom he had 52 sons. According to a tradition widely prevalent in Eastern Bundelkhand, Chhatrasal had fifty-two and a half *auras* sons. The historical record concerning his principal wife and chief queen (*patrani*) Devkunwar, is quite clear. The daughter of a Panwar chieftain, she was Chhatrasal's first wife whom he married at the age of eighteen. She pre-deceased him, leaving behind an only son, Hirdeshah, who, as heir-apparent (*pataut rajkumar*) succeeded Chhatrasal to the throne (*gaddi*) of Panna. Hirdeshah was the third, in order of birth, among Chhatrasal's sons. His second-born son, Jagatraj was born of a junior wife. Jagatraj's mother wanted her son to succeed Chhatrasal to the *gaddi* of Panna, but, in a letter to Jagatraj, the Raja himself expounded the principle of succession, based on the status of his marital union with the senior queen as superseding seniority in the order of birth of his sons. (Panna Letter no. 8). Chhatrasal carved out the *rajya* of Jaitpur from his own conquered territories, as bequest for Jagatraj. His other *auras* sons were also suitably provided for in the will.

The half-son in the tradition is believed to be the son of a prostitute who had once held Chhatrasal by the hand. In acknowledgement of that relationship, says the tradition, the Raja had honoured her by accepting the paternity of her male child. The tradition is too fragmentary to offer a satisfactory interpretation of the fact that Chhatrasal should have recognised *auras* in this 'son' even by half; and my remarks are largely speculative. The case is interesting because it represents the point of transition between two main categories of sons—the *auras* and *munhabole* (sons spoken of as such)—of Raja Chhatrasal. The principle of 'sonship' in the first category is genetic-cum-affinal. The principle in the second category, as we shall see, is political. However, clanship, affinity, and politics are brought together for reproduction and production in this milieu under the ideological umbrella of sacred (and magical) kingship. Clanship and affinity, on the one hand, and politics, on the other, can be seen as terms, in a complementary dualism, used to uphold the values of kingship. The son of the prostitute, in line with the sons of the first category, derives his rights (of patrimony) from the status of his mother's union with the father. But the status of the prostitute is precisely that of a public woman, and thus there is a connection between her son from the Raja and the sons of the political category. From the Raja's viewpoint, in relation to the *rajya*, he bestows ritual fatherhood upon the prostitute's son. This is because the position of the prostitute in the regional social system is ritualised. At the social level she represents the antithesis of the housewife. The worst abuse that may be directed against a married woman is to call her a *berni*. The social organisation of the Beria community (female, Berni) is an exact structural inversion of the patrilineal Rajput organisation. At the mythological level, however, the Goddess Lakshmi (an honorific substitute or qualifier for the housewife) belongs to the same class as *vesya* (the generic Sanskrit term for prostitute; *berni* being the regional representation of the class in Bundelkhand).[4] Similarly, in explaining *rai*, the ritual dancing by the *berni* to the accompaniment of obscene songs, at the beginning and end of the harvest festival (and the worship of Navadurga), my informants commented upon the aspect of homology between *Sati* (the epitome of virtuous wife) and *Vesya*. Both are *pativrata* (vowed to a single Lord)—the former to her husband, and the latter to God. In the course of my inquiries in the Beriya ward of Bijawar town, I was told that the prostitutes among the Berni still preserve the custom of the 'ritual marriage' of a girl to the man who deflowers her. He presents her with a piece of jewellery as a token of their special relationship. I have mentioned earlier the possible equation of land with the female principle in the generative ideology of the Bundelas. The king as *Bhupati* (Lord of the Land), stands as a bridegroom. The Berni as the dancer of *rai* at the harvest, is the public bride. When it is noted that *rai* is also the name given to the king's share of the produce from land (from *rai, raiyat*), and that Chhatrasal himself measures his prowess (*parakrama*) by the land he has 'done under him' (*jagha ki hai*), there seems little doubt that the 'fiction of *auras*' (thus ½ *auras*) in Chhatrasal's son from the prostitute is an acknowledgement of the bridegroom king's symbolic marriage with the bride of the land (territory-cum-people). At the same time the recognition of *auras* in the king's son conceived of a prostitute, provides the ritual legitimisation of the widest limits of exogamy (the unit of exogamy for a Bundela ruler) if the emphasis is shifted from the status of the spouse to territorial limit.

Before passing on to the category of Chhatrasal's political sons, it is essential to dispose of the question of wife-giving by the royal line. The standard Bundela genealogy does not register women. From local traditions it is clear that, as the sons, so also were the daughters of the *raja* classified into different grades, according to the class of their mother's union with the father. The mode of giving royal daughters away in marriage shows this. An interesting feature here is that all daughters of the raja's *auras* from the principal and junior wives were given away as clan daughters to the men of appropriate rank belonging to the other two clans of the Bundelkhandi Rajput grouping. So long as the raja's son-in-law was a Rajput by clanship (Panwar or Dhandhera, or exceptionally, from amongst the 36 kuri), kinship or pseudo-kinship (a Thakur), he stood on a status-equality footing with the raja's clan and kin. At this level there existed a generalised sentiment of brotherhood (*bhaiya-bandi*) amongst the regional dominants. But the rank of particular patrilines, families and individuals within the marriage class, could vary in proportion to their control of territory and/or military prowess. In choosing sons-in-law a Bundela Raja or Thakur would have to assess the political potential of the alliance. Patrilines, families and individuals with established domains ranked higher than those with little territory and these, in turn, ranked higher than those with military potential alone. However, the rank of families and individuals was not immutable. To the extent that particular men of the brotherhood status showed promise of military leadership, the wife-givers could materially upgrade their rank by the gift of a suitable land dowry. As a rule, the daughters from the principal wife and the junior wives were given as principal and junior wives to the Rajas and Thakurs of the first two grades. The daughters from subsidiary wives were given away as subsidiary wives.

On account of this function of land-dowry, the family and antecedents of his principal wife were the surest indicators of a Thakur's own rank. Thus, while the author of *Chhatraprakas* has nothing whatever to say about the Panwar raja, whose daughter the hero Chhatrasal married as his principal wife, we hear him mention that 'His (Chhatrasal's) mother-in-law was of illustrious descent' (Pogson 1828:46). To this day, my Bundela informants of Basari village (former Panna *rajya*) laid great stress on making discreet enquiries about a girl's *mamiawara* (her mother's patrilineage) before settling a match. Women in this society are not so much the bearers of ritual purity that they appear to be in a caste system; as principal wives their function is to indicate the political rank of patrilines, families and individuals in a clan system.

At the extreme end of the spectrum, the gift of the prostitute's daughter, Mastani, by Chhatrasal to the Maratha Peshwa Balaji Bajirao, offers an interesting case. In the subsequent period, Bundela rajas are known to have given away the female off-spring of their concubines (kept women or *rakhail*) as part of a daughter's dowry. However, what makes the tradition of gifting Mastani special, is that she is believed to have been the daughter of a prostitute (public woman) from the *auras* of

Chhatrasal. Furthermore, she was given away to the Peshwa to forge an important political alliance of pseudo-kinship between the Bundelas and the Marathas. The significance of the gift of the king's daughter, born of a prostitute, has been blurred by the subsequent controversy as to whether Mastani's mother was a Muslim. To my mind, no such contention about the religion of a Bundelkhandi prostitute would have arisen, had not the son, born to Balaji Bajirao (a Maratha) from her daughter, been initiated as a Muslim into the Peshwa's court at Poona. From the viewpoint of an indigenous political system based on generalised kinship, Mastani appears to be the female counterpart of the half son of Chhatrasal. While the king's son from the prostitute may be seen to mediate the agnatic contradiction (between *auras* sons and political sons), his daughter from the bride-of-the-land mediates the affinal contradiction (between wife-takers of the Rajput brotherhood and non-Rajput wife-takers). The sexless issue (eunuch) of a Thakur was fit to be given as a gift to a Muslim.

Pseudo-kinship

Yet, in a kinship system without a positive marriage rule and a corresponding categorical distinction between agnates and affines, there exist several choices in the assimilation and classification of outsiders as kin. The choices most frequently made in establishing pseudo-kinship by the royal line of the Bundelas were those of son/father, son/mother, and brother/brother. Except for the son/mother category which on the face of it, appears uterine, the rest are agnatic and must be explained in terms of Bundela clanship. According to a native Bundela historian, Chhatrasal acknowledged 12 *munhabole bete* (literally, 'sons spoken of as such'; my category of 'political sons' in addition to his fifty-two *auras* sons (Kunwar Kanhaiyaju 1928).

Two or three of these sons were ascetics (presumably Gosain), whom Chhatrasal won back from renunciation to the life of householders and soldiers. The ancestors of the Rajas of Maihar (a Jogi) and Bijairaogarh in Baghelkhand (east of zone 3) are reputed to have been from this lot. The castes of his other political sons are given as Ghosi, Brahmin, Bania, Bhat and Khawas (barber in royal service). It is clear that they were adopted irrespective of their place in the ritual hierarchy. In the native Bundela ideology even Peshwa Bajirao (whom as a 'taker' of Chhatrasal's daughter one can classify as a son-in-law) is seen as a political son of Chhatrasal. According to a native Bundela historian, the gift of Mastani was only a means of establishing the father/son kinship between the Bundela king and the Maratha Peshwa, and there is direct documentary proof (the Panna Letter Collections) that this is how the relationship was conceived and carried on even after the death of Chhatrasal. Kunwar Kanihaiyaju's (1928) hero (Chhatrasal), explains how the gift of Mastani will establish the filial bond between the two rulers:

> Sons are of two kinds. One kind is that which is produced from own blood. The other kind is obtained by giving a daughter (Ibid. 1928).

Here we see clearly how the agnatic kinship idiom is employed so as to make affinity subserve the interests of an indigenous clan polity.

The employment of a uterine category (son/mother) appears at first sight quite unexpected in a milieu of agnatic and patrilineal pseudo-kinship. The local tradition which fits this category is as follows: On hearing of the fame of Maharaja Chhatrasal, a poet (*bhat*) from Delhi chose to settle down in Mau (the capital of Chhatrasal before the founding of Panna). As fate would have it (*daivayoga se*), he died in his youth. For his beautiful wife, this separation was a cruel blow which drove her to desperation. Maharaja Chhatrasal had made a public pronouncement that throughout his kingdom if a girl from Bundelkhand had been married to a man who lived within the region, she should not cover her face in his presence since she was like his own daughter. Now, one day, this widow sent a letter to Maharaja Chhatrasal:

> Thou who art endowed with all the qualities, the Protector of Subjects, (*prajapalak*), the Succour of Clan [*kuladhayak*], the 108 Maharaja Chhatrsalji, I am an unfortunate, unhappy widow. I entreat you to grace my hut with your presence so that I may narrate to you my tale of woe. I remain solicitous of your kindness. Your bond-servant (*dasi*), Pyaribai Bhatan [the wife of a Bhat].

Chhatrasal assured the letter bearer that he would visit the hut of Pyaribai Bhatan. Subsequently, when, one day he happened to pass by Pyaribai's house, he stopped his coach, and ordered the widow to narrate her tale. With folded hands Pyaribai said she would like to speak with him in private. The king went upto the doorstep, but the widow spoke from inside the house, begging him to cross the threshold and come in. The king thought, 'Perhaps she wants to show me her dilapidated house and secure my orders for its repair'. He went in. The widow took him to the sleeping quarters (*chitsari*). There she said, 'O King, I am well-endowed with grain and wealth. Passion (*kama*) torments me. I wish the gift of a son from you.' The king thought to himself, 'What a calamity this is! (*Bahut anartha hua!*)' He asked her why she wanted a son from him. Pyaribai replied that if she were given this gift, she would desire nothing more in the world. Just as she said this, the king took her breast and began to suckle it. Then he stood up with folded hands and said, 'Mother, I am your son. I wait on your orders.' Thereafter, he transported her, in the royal coach to his palace where his own mother also lived.[5] It was only after the two women had bathed and eaten, that the king ate his own food. (Translated from the Hindi text narrated by Thakur Raja Ram Singh Bundela of Sendpa village, Chhatarpur district on 5 November 1971).

At the beginning of the story, the widow, a girl in his kingdom, has the pseudo-kinship status of being the Raja's daughter. The incest taboo stands between the King and the Bhatan's request for the gift of a son from him. (Unlike the prostitute she cannot be the bride-of-the-land to the bridegroom king.) But the situation which confronts the chief of the Bundela royal line is not unusual. As we have noted earlier, the unit of endogamy for the Bundela draw him dangerously close to incest. The solution is strictly homologous to the solution institutionalised in the dominant Bundela patrilines, namely, the recognition by pseudo-kinship of the surrogate milk-line of the Dauwa. The transformation of the milk-motherhood of the Bhatan widow (apparently a uterine relationship), to agnation with the surrogate milk-line, is brought about by the Bundelas themselves. My informant remarked that the Bhat political sons of Chhatrasal claim their kinship (brotherhood) with the Bundelas with reference to Chhatrasal having established the mother/son relationship with Pyaribai. Here again, just as in the case of the Dauwa and the Marathas, we find that to whatever non-agnatic categories these traditions of pseudo-kinship might at first sight appear to belong, their teleological nexus with clanship remains dominant.

A Note on Caste and Sect

This account of Chhatrasal's political sons shows clearly the extremely wide limits of Bundela exogamy, which crosses over to inter-caste relations. The popular and extra-caste nature of Chhatrasal's allies in rural Bundelkhand, is explicitly described in the poetic biography, *Chhatraprakasa* by Lal Kavi. In considering his political sons, it is clear that the lower limits of Bundela Rajput caste were shadowy, merging with 'lower' castes of Bhat and Khawas, the ascetic castes like Gosain and Jogi and middle and higher castes, viz., Bania and Brahmin. Chhatrasal's deviation from caste orthodoxy and his intimate relations with other castes (some higher than the Rajput but mostly lower ones), is thus described (M.P. Singh 1973: 99-100): Among the 25 persons who stood by Chhatrasal during the organisation of his militia were:

1. Kunwar Naraindas (Bundela)
2. Govindrai (Bundela)
3. Sundarmani (Panwar)
4. Dalsingar (Dauwa)
5. Rammani (Dauwa)
6. Meghraj (Parihar)

7. Dhurmangad (Bagsi)
8. Kisori (Khangar)
9. Prabal (Mishra)
10. Lachhe or Sawat (Rawat)
11. Bhan (Bhat)
12. Maghi dayal
13. Haribans
14. Pawal (Dhimar)
15. Kharga (Bari)
16. Modi (Teli)

Most indigenous historians and commentators cite the above as proof of Chhatrasal's campaigns being rooted in the popular folk consciousness (*jana manas*). They also recount events in the early life of their hero when he became an orphan at the age of 12 years (Singh 1975: 84-86). It is said that during his early wanderings, as the son of his deceased father and nobleman, Champat Rai, Chhatrasal went to see their priest (purohit), named Bhan. However, the latter, in view of our hero's penury, would have nothing to do with his *jajman*. On the other hand, people of a more lowly caste and occupation, like the daughter of Baradia Kumhar (potter) from Nunha village, the old Lallu Gadariya (shepherd) from the same village and Mahabali Teli (oil-presser) from Dailwara village gave their support, sustenance and encouragement to the forlorn Chhatrasal.

Correlated with the heroic disdain of the high caste is the importance of sect in the kingship of Panna, exemplified by Chhatrasal's career. The prime example of a charismatic sectarian leader, of course, is Swami Prannath of the Pranami sect. Besides the coronation of Chhatrasal and the ritual of tying him with the sword of kingship on Dussehra day, Prannath led him to the vast treasure of diamonds in Panna. The conjunction of kingship with the treasure-trove effected by the charismatic swami is epitomised in a saying which the people of Bundelkhand repeat to this day:

Chhatta tere raj mein dharni dhak dhak hoye,
Jit Jit ghora mukh kare, tit tit fatteh hoye.

(Chatta, i.e., Chhattrasal, the land of your kingdom vibrates with the glow of diamonds; whichever way your stallion turns, in that very direction will your kingdom spread.)

The Treaty of Bassein between the Marathas and the British East India Company in 1801, laid the foundations of a political system which was to last for the next one hundred and fifty years. The British dispensation in Bundelkhand rested on the military subjugation of the Marathas and the Bangash Nawab of Farrukhabad, and the legal restoration of a segementary state structure among Rajput chiefs. From the inception of British paramountcy in the early nineteenth century, one can clearly trace the process by which law substituted custom, and caste substituted kinship as regulating principles of the indigenous political system. The transition, as might be expected, was full of conflict. The rebellion of 1857 in Bundelkhand was an outcome of this contradictory situation. In the post-mutiny period, however, due in large measure to the growth of a monopolistic money economy, and the increasing stratification within the ruling class, the British succeeded in creating legalistic socio-economic grades in Bundelkhand, detaching the class of chiefs and their families from that of cultivating commoners. Thus, towards the close of the nineteenth century one might look upon the families and houses of native chiefs as constituting a regional level distinct from the lineage-based cultivating commoners at the local level of the political system. In this changed political and economic setting, what could no longer be achieved by kinship and custom was effected by legal provisions, especially by the paramount control of civil law pertaining to land ownership. The redefinition of social dominance was bound to have serious repercussions on the structure of agrarian class relations.

Notes

1. Contraray to Mayer's report (1965) on the Malwa Rajputs (of 36 kuri) the mother's brother in the Bundelkhand Rajput grouping is not included in the *khandan*.

2. A delineation of the classification of marital unions and concubinage, from the point of view of the woman involved in them, will take us far outside the main theme of this discussion. Instructive comparisons may be drawn between the institution of Berni (religious 'prostitutes' of Bundelkhand) and the Devdasi and Basavi and between the Nambudiri-Nayar relationship in Kerala with the Bundela-Dauwa league in Bundelkhand.
3. A commentary on the 'partition of heritage' in Hindu Law composed by Mitra Misra under the direction of Bir Singh Dev, Bundela ruler of Orchha from 1606 to 1630 AD.
4. The mythological allusion is to an event of no smaller magnitude than the creation of the universe itself by the churning of the primeval ocean. Of the fourteen products of the churning, both Lakshmi and Vesya fell to the lot of the gods (*deva*) who countenanced the demons in a fierce combat.
5. This must refer to a secondary wife of his father, Champat Rai, since both his father and mother were killed before Chhatrasal had attained youth.

Chapter IV

Marriage Alliance in Bundelkhand: Hardaul as the Male Affine

The primary reference of the legend of Hardaul is to the dynastic phase and the secondary reference is to the mythological, legendary and dominance phases of Bundela genealogy. Given this wide reference span, it is apparently the most complete of Bundela legends. The formation, in Bundelkhand, of a female cult around the principal character of this legend, its wide geographic distribution in association with the cholera epidemic from Bundelkhand to Punjab (Crooke 1974), and the diversity of folklore forms into which it has passed, mark it out as the most popular of Bundela legends.

Smith (1875: 389) provides the following summary of this legend, which is the only one available in English translation:

> Hardaul, a son of the famous Bir Singh Bundela of Orchha, was born at Datiya. His brother, Jhajhar Singh (Jhujhar Singh) suspected him of undue intimacy with his wife, and at a feast poisoned him with all his followers. After this tragedy, it happened that the daughter of Kunjavati, the sister of Jhajhar and Hardaul, was about to be married. Kunjavati, accordingly sent an invitation to Jhajhar Singh, requesting him to attend the wedding. He refused, and mockingly replied that she had better invite her favourite brother, Hardaul. Thereupon she went in despair to his tomb and lamented aloud. Hardaul from below answered her cries, and said that he would come to the wedding and make all arrangements. The ghost kept his promise, and arranged the nuptials as befitted

the honour of his house. Subsequently, he visited, at night, the bedside of Akbar, and besought the emperor to command *chabutras* (platforms) to be erected and honour paid him in every village throughout the empire, promising that, if he were duly honoured, a wedding should never be marred by storm or rain, and that no one who first presented a share of his meal to Hardaul should ever want for food. Akbar complied with these requests, and since that time Hardaul's ghost has been worshipped in every village. He is chiefly honoured at weddings and in Baisakh (April-May), during which month women, especially of the lower castes, visit his *chabutra* and eat there. His *chabutra* is always built outside the village. On the day but one before the arrival of a wedding procession, the women of the family worship the gods and Hardaul, and invite them to the wedding. If any sign of a storm appears, Hardaul is propitiated with songs.

We may divide the above summary into four episodes:

1. The poisoning of a younger brother (Hardaul) by the elder brother (Jujhar Singh), the ruler of Orchha.
2. The role of the ghost of Hardaul at the wedding of the daughter of his sister (Kunjavati).
3. The role of the Moghul emperor in promulgating the cult.
4. The establishment and character of the cult.

Episodes 1 and 2 refer to the legend, and 3 and 4 to the cult of Hardaul. In the following analysis I shall use two oral narratives of the legend, recorded by me in the villages of Kurra-Rampur and Sendpa, Bundela *jagirs* of the former kingdoms of Panna and Bijawar respectively, and three printed Hindi texts from Chhatarpur, Nowgong and Jhansi. The 'Song of Hardaul' reproduced in Hindi by Smith (1875: 390-92) is the only version I have from Datia.

Let me first establish the identity of Hardaul in the political and kinship contexts of the dynastic phase of Bundela genealogy. From the viewpoint of the regional political system, the carving out of the kingdoms of Chanderi and Datia was of crucial importance. Chanderi started as the seat of Ramshah, Bir Singh Deo's deposed elder brother. The fort of Datia was given by Bir

Singh Deo himself to his son, Bhagwan Rai. In the wider political context, by this time, the ruling house of Orchha had accepted the paramountcy of the Moghul emperor. The distribution of shares in the kingdom from Bhartichand received ratification from the Moghul emperor by the grant of a *sanad* (treaty of engagement) to the *rajas* (kings), and of *khillat* (seal of office) to some of the *jagirdars* (domain-holders). The subsequent incorporation of regional kings and dominants into the imperial system was affected by the grant of *mansabs* over territories under direct imperial rule, in recognition of the distinguished services rendered by particular members of Bundela royalty and nobility. Formally, therefore, the regional political system at this point of time had become a subordinate part of the imperial hierarchy. Thus, down to the level of the *jagirdars* there was a possibility of direct links with the Emperor in Delhi, although by far, the majority of *jagirs* were still granted independently by the regional *rajas*. The Moghul court recognised Orchha, from which the other kingdoms and *jagirs* now branched out, as the pre-eminent Bundela royal house of the regional political system. Nevertheless, the extent to which the Emperor consulted the Raja of Orchha in regional political affairs depended in practice on the degree of loyalty shown to him by this raja. Unlike the Hindu kings of Rajputana, however, the Bundela royalty had not, in general, tried to ingratiate themselves with the Emperor by sending their women to his harem.[1] The subsequent history of regional political systems shows that this matrimonial exclusiveness of the Bundelas, matched by the insularity and inaccessibility of their terrain, made for a greater measure of political autonomy of the Bundela rajas, as compared to their western counterparts in Rajasthan. It enabled the regional rajas and adventurers to participate strategically in the wars of succession for the throne of Delhi. Bir Singh Deo's rise to power in Bundelkhand is directly attributable to his strategic alliance with Prince Salim (later Emperor Jahangir) on the eve of Akbar's death. But in his later years, Bir Singh Deo quarrelled with his patron. A similar fluctuation in the relationship between the Bundela rajas and the

Emperor is reflected incessantly throughout the course of medieval Bundelkhand history.

Raja Bir Singh Deo of Orchha had 12 sons from three queens. He distributed shares to his sons and grandsons within his lifetime. Jhujhar Singh, the eldest son by the senior queen, was nominated heir apparent and successor. Hardaul, the fifth in chronological order among the children of Bir Singh Deo by his second queen, chose to serve his father at Orchha as Prime Minister (Diwan) of the kingdom. He is said to have refused the offer of a substantial *jagir*, although Baragaon village (tehsil Baldeogarh), was subsequently made over to him by Bir Singh Deo in recognition of his administrative and military services to the kingdom. Diwan Hardaul continued to reside in Orchha as Prime Minister during the early part of the reign of his half-brother, Jhujhar Singh, as well.

The eldest of the full siblings of Hardaul was Bhagwan Rao, the ruler of Datia. While Datia occupies a prominent place in the legend of Hardaul, Bhagwan Rao is conspicuously absent from all its versions. The reason seems to be that along with two of his sons, Bhagwan Rao, stayed at the Emperor's court as his father's representative. It was only a year before Bir Singh Deo's death that he moved to Datia and took possession of Baroni, allotted for the maintenance of his father. On the one hand, he quarrelled with Jhujhar Singh over the question of succession, and on the other hand, his own son, Dhurmangad, stayed in Orchha while his father and two half brothers were away in Delhi, and usurped the full share of the kingdom (the *jagir* of Palera), allotted to him (Bhagwan Rao) by Bir Singh Deo. In the animosity between the Bundelas of Orchha and Datia, therefore, Bhagwan Rao's own full bother Hardaul, and his son Dhurmangad, seem to have joined the adversary.

From the perspective of Bundela royal agnation by membership of the patrilineage, all the sons of Bir Singh Deo belonged to Orchha. With the political fission of the Datia ruling house from Orchha, the identification of Hardaul with Orchha, both as Prime Minister of Orchha and *jagirdar* of Baragaon (in Jatara *pargana*, south-east of the capital of the

Budhoo Gadaria of village Parsania preparing for being the 'horse' *(ghoda)* of a deceased Thakur during the *yatra* at Deepavali

Cenotaphs *(makbara)* of deceased Thakurs in village Bhagwan

A monument *(chabutara)* to commemorate Maharaj Chhatrasal in Chhatarpur town

A Sati monument near village Sendpa

kingdom) is retained. But merging lineage segmentation and political fission tell us only a part of the story, and account satisfactorily only for those versions which address their hero as Diwan Hardaul, the prince of Orchha. There is another version, by far the most popular in Bundeli folklore, where the hero is called 'Lala Hardaul'. Now 'Lala' is a term of address for a male affine. In the structure of the narrative, the derivation of this title for Hardaul is obviously from his special relationship as husband's younger brother (*devar*) to the queen of Jhujhar Singh, his elder brother's wife (*bhauji*). In this particular reference, the title 'Lala Hardaul' is commensurate with the hero's identity as Diwan, and Prince of Orchha.

However, what is significant is that in all those versions where Hardaul is identified with Datia, as being born there or commanding a host therefrom (Smith 1875), he is *always* referred to as Lala to the *exclusion* of his title Diwan. Obviously, this has little to do with his membership of the Bundela 'sublineage' of Datia with his full-brother, Bhagwan Rao, the ruler of Datia, as its head. As I have said earlier, Bhagwan Rao never makes an appearance in the legend, even in those versions which identify Hardaul with Datia. To explain this regularity (Lala and Datia, Lala and Orchha, but Lala and Datia excluding Diwan and Orchha) we have to locate the significance of Hardaul historically in the territorial context of the league of intermarriage between the Bundela, the Dhandhera and the Panwar; and structurally in the kin-category 'male affine'.

Accounts of royal intermarriage from the state records of Orchha and Datia help us piece together but a fragmentary picture, with many gaps. The senior queen of Bir Singh Deo and the *raja mata* (queen mother) of Orchha in the reign of Jhujhar Singh, was his own mother, Amrit Kunwari, the daughter of Diwan Shyam Singh Dhandhera of Sahara-Shahabad. The Dhanderas of Sahara-Shahabad had given daughters to the Bundela royalty at Orchha in earlier generations as well. Both the mother and senior queen of Rudrapratap belonged to this family. The second queen of Bir Singh Deo, and mother of Hardaul (Baragaon), Bhagwan Rao (Datia),

Chandrabhan (Jaitpur, Kunch), Kishan Singh (Deoraha), and Kunjavati was Guman Kumari, the daughter of Singhaji Panwar of Kairwan.[2] For this set of siblings we have data for the marriages of Bhagwan Rao and his descendants of the Datia ruling house, and for the marriage of their sister Kunjavati. All these marriages took place with the Panwar to the virtual exclusion of the Dhandhera. There is some evidence of the antagonism between Bhagwan Rao, and Jhujhar Singh's (Dhandhera) mother as senior queen, over the claim to that status advanced by Bhagwan Rao's (Panwar) mother. (Luard, 1907: 95). Furthermore, the third and youngest queen of Bir Singh Deo was also a daughter of the Dhandhera of Sahara Shahbad. It would thus seem that each of the two primary factions formed by the lineal descendants of Bir Singh Deo not only had its leader and royal capital, but also its complement of marital allies; the Dhandhera for Orchha, and the Panwar for Datia.

However, the similarity between the two Bundela teams ends at the level of their formal structure. The role of their marital allies in the actual political process was uneven. Bhagwan Rao owed the formation of his kingdom at Datia to the support of the Panwar allies—initially to the Kairwan Panwars, the family of his own mother, and subsequently to those of his three queens, daughters, respectively of the Panwars of Barechha, Pali and Ambabagh. Of these, the family of his senior queen, the Panwars of Barechha, had a long history of marital alliance with Bundela royalty. Furthermore, Bhagwan Rao's own sister, Kunjavati, had been given in marriage to the same family, and two generations later, Bhagwan Rao's grandson Dalpat Rao, took a daughter from them. Bir Singh's Dhandhera allies had no comparable role to play in the political process at Orchha, since Jhujhar Singh had inherited an already consolidated kingdom.

Before returning to the legend, there is just one more point to be noted; the politically powerful affinal network of Panwar allies for the Bundela branch of Datia, and the comparative looseness, territorial fragmentation and weakness of this network for the Bundela branch of Orchha. For a comparison between the two Bundela kingdoms in these terms I shall again resort to the geo-political context and the principle of descent-based rule, which were first applied to a regional comparison between the ruling groups of Gwalior-Jalaun (set A) and Garhkundar-Orchha (set B) along a north-south axis. As a consequence of political fission in the Bundela dynasty at Orchha, the kingdoms of Datia and Orchha reappear as sub-sets A_1 and B_1 of A and B. A_1 shares many of the characteristics of set A—a western location, intermarrying local patrilineages, lack of a political frontier, and progressive division of power between, on the one hand, the local dominants and, on the other hand, the Moghul emperor. The Raja is very much a *primus inter pares* among the local dominants; whatever superior authority he has derived from a higher political power. Interposition by an alien regional power is also provided for in this system. Sub-set B_1 on the other hand, continues to share most of the relevant characteristics of B. Territorially, it retains a south-easterly direction, both in the context of consolidation through the spread of patrilineages of local dominants and the shifting capital of the Raja, and expansion through kingdom formation by political fission. The overt political control by a higher-level power is weak, and regional authority continues to be derived largely from the indigenous notion of descent-based rule. And yet, there is a fundamental similarity between A_1 and B_1, shared only partly by A and B. Etiologically, the similarity is derived from the common genetic base of A_1 and B_1, namely, the filiation of both to the Bundela dynasty of Orchha, which itself rests on the principle of clanship. The legend of Hardaul helps us to discern the common ideological superstructure, which transcends overt differences in the socio-political processes of Orchha and Datia. It also brings us to the structural counterpart of historical analysis.

In the historical perspective, the position of our hero, Hardaul, is anomalous. By proximity of unilineal descent he belongs to Datia, and is spoken of as such in the Datia version of the legend and in the summary given by Smith. By political affiliation, as office and jagir holder, he belongs to Orchha.

Another anomaly is revealed by the two kinds of sources, historical and legendary, with regard to Hardaul's marriage and progeny. His marriage is assumed in the dynastic history of Orchha, which shows that Hardaul's male descendants, who first held Baragaon and Digaura, actually supplied cadets for succession by adoption to the ruling line of Orchha. All versions of the legend, on the other hand, systematically 'forget' about Hardaul's own marriage and progeny. Why should this be so? In the first place, Jhujhar Singh does not kill his brother by poisoning him at a public feast: having been led to suspect adultery between Hardaul and his queen, he importunes her to cook and serve poisoned food to her brother-in-law in the kitchen of their living quarters. Moreover, the connection made in Smith's summary between the legend (episodes 1 and 2), and the cult (episodes 3 and 4), is not borne out by indigenous sources. For Smith, episode 3—the promulgation of the cult by order of the Emperor—is crucial;[3] while the cult's female character is mentioned by him in passing. What Smith has failed to notice is that both the legend and the cult are primarily about women, although the legend itself, because of Hardaul, is allowed to masquerade in male garb. The depiction of episodes 1 and 2 in indigenous sources permits us to invert the conventional male-dominated perspective of political history. Viewed as a female representation of Bundela ideology, the legend contains unexpected clues for explaining the anomalies and contradictions of the regional social structure.

If we reconstruct the kinship matrix of episode 1, the poisoning of Hardaul, the following set of relationships is obtained:

Elder brother—Younger brother
Husband (*raja*)—Wife (*rani*)
Elder brother's wife (*bhouji*)—Husband's younger brother (*devar*)

These relationships constitute the elementary semantic universe for the conscious interpretation of adultery and fratricide depicted in this episode. In the actual handling of these themes, however, the last of these relationships (*bhouji-devar*) is transformed into another, mother-son. The moral message of this transformation is obvious: to absolve Hardaul and the queen of the accusation of adultery by moving their potentially sexual relationship into the kin-category, circumscribed by the incest taboo. In some versions the same effect is achieved even more clearly, by depicting Hardaul in a state of pious celibacy (*brahmachari*). Both these would provide an easy answer to the question of the legend's amnesia about Hardaul's marriage and progeny. In terms of the Bundela ideology of descent, however, it is not so much the suppression of Hardaul's sexuality for his moral vindication that interests us, but the structural implications of transforming, an 'affinal' relationship into a 'consanguineal' one and, the double representation of 'affinity' in both the real relationship and that to which it has been transformed. Episode 2 serves to elucidate this issue.

In the rendering of episode 2, the role of Hardaul's ghost at the wedding of his sister's daughter reveals at once the intended meaning of this legend. The key kinship relations expressed overtly are those between a Bundela brother and sister and between Hardaul as mother's brother to his sister's children.[4]

In the interpretation of Hardaul's role as the gift-bearing mother's brother at the wedding of Kunjavati's daughter, two facts deserve to be noted. First, the ghost of Hardaul is invoked for the fulfillment of this role despite the presence of several full (e.g. Bhagwan Rao) and half (e.g. Jhujhar Singh) brothers of Kunjavati. This brings out the opposition between the living and the dead, with pre-eminence accorded to the latter. When it is remembered that Kunjavati's own husband, the Panwar Thakur of Barechha is also dead, the pre-eminence of the dead in the female cult of Hardaul alerts us to its affinal content. This impression receives further confirmation by a second feature of the legend and the cult—the continuing identity of Hardaul as '*lala*' (male affine). Even in those cult-songs which focus on episode 2 and go into the previous one only to sketch the biography of the Hero, the focal term of address (by female speakers) for Hardaul is not brother (*bhaiya*) or mother's brother (*mama*), but '*lala*'.

So far the meaning of territorial domain predominantly as *rajya* and *jagir*, has been outlined in the framework of political fission and agnatic segmentation in the ruling groups. I also mentioned that rulership by the Bundela branch of Datia (sub-set A_1) was embedded in the kinship network of repeated affinity with the Panwar dominants of western Bundelkhand. The relationship between territorial domain and inter-clan affinity during the dynastic phase of Bundela past deserves a closer look. The practice of granting revenue rights in villages as dowry (*dayja*) to royal sisters and daughters seems to have been general. Thus the Panwar and Dhandhera bride-takers of the Bundela rulers became their *jagirdars* and *sardars* as well. The class of these nobles and officials enjoying revenue-rights in Bundela kingdoms included both the bride-taking *and bride-giving* affines of the Panwar and Dhandhera clans. The Panwars and Dhandheras were also retainers in the armies of rulers; at the primary level these were the native rajas and at the secondary and paramount levels these were the Maratha *peshwas* and the Moghul emperors. Our concern is with the ties of these Rajputs with primary rulers alone. In this relationship they held territorial-cum-revenue rights of the Bundela rajas either through affinity or military service, but usually by both kinds of linkages. Furthermore, particular Panwar and Dhandhera lineages (territorially designated) held jagirs under more than one ruler, i.e., Bundela 'brothers' who were rulers of separate kingdoms. The role of the affines was based on their *kinship status* as allies rather than on any supposed permanency of their subordinate *political status* as *jagirdars* and *sardars* of Bundela rajas. Only a minority of the affines of Bundela rajas, those who had adopted uxorilocal residence following a marital 'domain gift', became politically subordinate to the donor branch. The majority continued to live in their western territories of Gwalior and Malwa. They retained a large degree of freedom for strategic participation in wider political conflicts. Taking advantage of their multiple links with the Bundela rajas, they augmented their martial resources by predatory exploits. Right up to the end of the eighteenth century, nowhere in Bundelkhand did the Panwar and the Dhandhera form their own kingdoms. In alliance with the Bundelas, their power was of a mercenary and predatory character. In the setting of Bundela rule during the dynastic phase, the concept of stratified lineages with a vertical or pyramidal model for the distribution of power gives us a lop-sided view of the political system. The horizontal 'Rajput' linkages of the ruling group in Bundelkhand were circumscribed in the first place by the exogamic rule of intermarriage between the three clans. The rule operated in a geo-political context which defined the power-base of the Bundelas differently from that of their Panwar and Dhandhera allies. The descent base of Bundela rule emphasised clanship. In practical terms, the political expansion of the Bundelas has resulted in a situation of dispersed clanship over a large territory. During the dynastic phase Bundela polity had also inherited the structure of enmity between brothers as its essential feature. Expectedly, therefore, the political facet of what was basically a kinship alliance between the Bundela and their marital allies, reflects the quarrel between the brothers. But episode 2 of the legend of Hardaul shows not only the breach but also its resolution. The conflict between the brothers, mediated by their affines, is resolved by the cementing of the dispersed clanship of the Bundelas. This, I submit, is the essential framework for an interpretation of Hardaul, the hero of a female cult of the dead, with his legendary identity combining in one character, the roles of younger brother, mother's brother, and male affine.

Two details of the legend illustrate the above propositions in a striking manner. What Smith has erroneously taken to suggest the poisoning of Hardaul at a public feast is a fact alluded to in all indigenous versions, namely, the death of 900 (the figure varies) of Hardaul's soldiers following their General's eating of poisoned food. The dead soldiers form part of a series of deadly calamities which befell birds, beasts, a loyal Basor (sweeper), and others, due to the supernatural disorder caused by the hero's treacherous murder. It is noteworthy, however, that the only version that gives a social identity to Hardaul's soldiers, describes them as Panwar. This piece of information fits in with the mercenary and predatory character of the Bundelas' marital and martial allies of the other two clans discussed earlier, and with the evidence we have about the Datia Bundelas' strong alliance with the Panwar in their rivalry with the kingdom of Orchha. More generally, it illustrates the structural-historical location of the ruling group's marital allies between hostile royal brothers.

The second detail pertains to the end of episode 2. It illustrates the structural interposition of marital alliance to cement the dispersed clanship of the Bundelas. The ghost of Hardaul is by now tamed by the ministration of females—Hardaul's sister Kunjavati (widow of the Panwar Thakur of Barechha), her daughter (to be married to a Bundela bridegroom of Chamal village), and Jhujhar Singh's wife (with whom Kunjavati affirms a bond of solidarity on the occasion of visiting Hardaul's tomb at Orchha by inviting her to attend the wedding in the role of *mami* or mother's brother's wife). Female magic completes the transition from the stage of agnatic solidarity between Hardaul, (when he is still alive), and his brother, to a stage where the breach between the brothers is underscored (the poisoning of Hardaul), and finally to the point where Hardaul's ghost appears in its uterine-affinal aspect. The last stage of the transition is brought about by a loud lamentation by Kunjavati at Hardaul's tomb where she utters a powerful curse on the living as opposed to the dead: '*jitan pe gajen parain, marai sudharo kaj*' (May the living be struck by lightning and the dead take charge of affairs!). The merging of Hardaul with the dead is not fortuitous but an essential characteristic of his power as the tutelary spirit of a female cult. A praise-song from Datia vests Hardaul with demonical powers; '*jalmat khaye gotiya, hot khaye mai-bap*' (You, who ate up your clansmen at birth, and soon thereafter your mother and father.) In this song, furthermore, the father (with the clansmen) is eaten up and forgotten but the brother and sister (Hardaul and Kunjavati) affirm their solidarity by recalling how their mother was cremated on a pyre of sandalwood.

The power of the female expressed through the ghost as its symbol, like all symbols, is multivocal and the affinal notes of this symbol deserve to be recorded. As early as in her curse on the living, Kunjavati exhorts the ghost of her favourite brother to 'take charge of affairs'—manifestly, to perform the ritual role of the mother's brother at her daughter's wedding and latently, in the dominant opposition between the living and the dead, to be the 'ally' of her deceased husband. And, indeed, the call for alliance is imperative, for with Hardaul the obligation is both marital and martial (cf. the 900 Panwar soldiers who died with him). It follows, therefore, that the legend depicts the ghost of Hardaul as bringing gifts laden in bullock-carts to his niece's wedding and commanding a host (the deceased Panwar soldiers). These ghostly helpers are specifically opposed to those citizens of Datia whose offer of help is turned down by Kunjavati. Hardaul in Datia is thus the mother's brother in his affinal aspect, and a 'brother-in-death' of Kunjavati's deceased husband, the Panwar thakur of Barechha. This symbolic inversion of Hardaul's identity from living, consanguineal, male-linked ties to dead, affinal, and female-linked ties, constitutes the crux of the relationship between episodes 1 and 2 of the legend.

As a ghost, Hardaul becomes territorially mobile. He 'appears', first as a voice underneath his tomb in Orchha, then as a powerful disturbance in the bedroom of the Moghul emperor at Shahjahanabad, and again several times at his sister's daughter's wedding in Datia. There he manifests in the form of a crack in the pillar which would then be tied up with the ritual garment (*cikat*) to be donned by his niece, as a hand that serves food to the guests, and gives parting gifts to the bridegroom. However, the ghost it is, who also 'takes' the merit of the 'gift of the virgin' (*kanyadan*) and gives away five villages in *tika* to the bridegroom. It is worthwhile noting that this exchange takes place between clansmen (Hardaul and the Bundela bridegroom from Chamal). The names of the villages given by Hardaul are remembered by all those who know the legend well, but their history of changing land-rights is neither recalled nor considered relevant. The reality of the gift is rendered negatively and symbolically; in these villages alone there is no platform or seat (*chabutra*) erected in the memory of Hardaul. To this extent the five villages lie outside the domain of the ghost's power. The asymmetrical exchange between the two Bundelas, mediated by the Panwar bride, represents a symbolic reversal of Hardaul's identity from brotherhood by affinity back to brotherhood by agnation. The conflict between brothers (the context of lineage segmentation) when mediated by the allies (the context of affinity), is resolved by a symbolic exchange between them (the context of clanship).

The osmosis between Hardaul's identities as mother's brother (*mama*) and male affine (*lala*) in the legend, and the relationship of this uterine-affinal identity wth his agnatic identity as younger brother (to the ruler of Orchha) and clan brother (to his sister's daughter's husband), constitute a structural paradigm for locating the significance of alliance in the Bundela kinship system. This must be the subject of a separate study. What I hope is demonstrated by the study of this legend is the meaning and structural significance of clanship in Bundela rule during the dynastic phase. More specifically, I have argued that Hardaul as the hero of a female cult of the dead in Bundelkhand explicates the alliance counterpart of descent-based ideology in indigenous rule. It is the descent-construct *bans*, translated as 'clan' rather than as 'lineage', which enables us to encompass both the Bundela ideology and the processes of alliance during their dynastic past. With some simplification it may even be argued that the breach between brothers on the point of royal succession[5] (a phenomenon of ruling lineage) was counterbalanced by the intermarrying league of the three clans. As a limiting case of alliance based on clan exogamy, this league not only cemented the dispersed clanship of the Bundela but also regulated the process of .their expansion by political fission. Returning to the legend of Hardaul, its amnesia concerning the marriage and progeny of the hero is made intelligible by its internal function of resolving the agnatic conflict. The *generalisation* of the female cult of Hardaul throughout Bundelkhand belongs to the same genre as *sati* in central India, a transformation of the anti-political phenomenon (female-dominated, death-defined) to the cosmological plane. Viewed from the perspective of contemporary male-dominated *realpolitik*, the episode of Hardaul is cited by ex-royal Bundelas as a prime example of the discord between brothers. But the idiom in which this message is expressed supports, by its inversion, my analysis of the male affine placed as a hinge between the dispersed clanship of the Bundelas: '*Bundela bans bhaiyya ka meet nahin hota*' (The Bundela clan is not a friend of brothers).[6]

Notes

1. The only case known to me is that of Bhagwan Rao, Bundela Raja of Datia, who sent his sister (or daughter) into the imperial harem of Shahjahan.
2. The Panwar sublineages intermarrying with the Bundelas are believed to have descended from the four sons of Punyapal Panwar (see p. 14). Each is designated the domain of a son: thus from Ratansah, the Panwar of Karera; from Jetsah the Panwar of Kairwan; from Shandarshah, the Panwar of Barchha; from Chandrahansa (an illegitimate son of a prostitute named Chandrabhaga), the Panwar of Ghati Mayapur.
3. Smith's assertion that the Emperor intervened in that capacity following a request by Hardual's ghost is sheer nonsense in the light of indigenous versions. There the emperor is shown to order the building of *chabutras* in honour of Hardual throughout the land in a bid to placate Hardual's ghost, following a terrible visitation by him to the Emperor while he was asleep. Smith's reaction is yet another example of the 'premise of paramountcy' that plagued colonialist historiography in India.
4. In the context of the marriage of the sister's child (daughter)—a mother's brother is obliged to gift the *cikat* or *bhat*. The ritual (*neg*) of this presentation precedes the arrival of the groom's marriage party. The crucial gift is a dress brought by the mother's brother to be worn by his neice (*bhanejan*). The bringing of this gift itself is preceded by an invitation sent to the brother by the sister, with the accompaniment of white uncooked rice. Besides the ceremonial dress for the sister's child (*cikat*), the gifts include presents for the sister, her husband, her husband's parents, her husband's sisters, and the wives of her husband's brothers.

5. The crisis of royal succession during this period looks both backwards and forwards. I have already referred to the succession of Jhujhar Singh which was disputed by Bhagwan Rao of Datia, Bir Singh Deo's son from his Panwar queen. The forward-looking counterpart is provided in local histories. According to Munshi Harnarain, Hardaul 'after his death appeared as a spirit and revealed to many that Jhujhar Singh had poisoned him to prevent his succession, being himself childless.' (Silberrad 1902:115). Another historian (Kanhaiyaju) corroborates this impression by noting that Bir Singh Deo, in recognition of Hardual's services, had made the provision that his line would succeed to the throne of Orchha should the main line fail to produce heirs. It is noteworthy that Bundela royal succession was not a matter of deciding between proximate generations but stipulated three generations (grandparents-grandchildren). This perspective is available in those songs of Hardual where his descent is traced from his grandfather; '*Madhukarshah, ke natia, Brisinghdeo ke put*' (grandson of Madhukarshah, son of Bir Singh Deo).
6. If one were to take a cue from the structuralist approach but contextualise it historically as we have done in this chapter, the following complementary dualisms can be posited:
   male–female
   consanguinity–affinity
   brothers–enemies
   living–dead.

CHAPTER V

Rural Bundelkhand: Aspects of Agrarian Social Stratification

In his book, *Studies in Agrarian Social Structure* Andre Beteille has repeatedly stated that social anthropologists can contribute to the study of agrarian class relations by devoting attention to the native terminology used in connection with the ownership, control, and use of land in rural areas. Besides emphasising relationships based on land, he also occasionally mentions that dominance in land relationships is followed by control over people. The latter set of controls is viewed primarily as belonging to the category of patron-client ties, where a deferential attitude by the clients towards their patrons may give them better security and give the patrons, the promise of support in political alignments. With specific regard to agrarian relations, this correlates with the fact that the landed classes are able to disengage themselves from manual labour which is done for them by those under their command, whether as tenants or as hired agricultural labourers. (We exclude from this characterisation, peasant farmers.) One explanation of this correlation offered by Beteille, is the imperative of status. Another, closely related one, is the arduousness involved in agricultural work depending on the crop-pattern, ecological conditions etc.

This chapter responds to Beteille's point about the significance of indigenous classifications for the study of agrarian relations. Such classifications can only be made in a specific local setting, and without prejudging the nature of social classes—either in open conflict or implicit contradictions. The task also requires a formal model of the relationship between land and labour which can subsume the possibilities of the typically Indian relationship between caste and class. Beteille's descriptive and disjunctive treatment of the variables of land, work, and status, in examining the phenomenon of agrarian relationships, is not aided by such a model.

The construction of such a model is helped by Leach's discussion of caste and class (Leach 1960:5-6). In a word, he may be considered to be proposing an hour-glass model of the caste system in contrast to a pyramidal model of the class system (Fig. 3: p. 99).

Leach characterises the caste system thus: (a) Numerically there are large populations at the top and at the bottom, with a minority of specialist castes in the middle. (b) Lower castes in the system have their rights, they have security. In the system as a whole, security and status are polarised. (c) The high-caste majority competes for the services of the middle-caste minority and low-caste workers. In contrast, he views a class system as typified by the following: (a) Numerically the upper classes constitute a minority and the lower classes, the majority (b) Lower classes have been pushed to the bottom by ruthless competition and—unlike the lower castes—have minimal security. In the class system as a whole, therefore, status and security go hand in hand. The numerically large lower classes compete for the favours of the numerically small upper classes.

It is obvious that in Leach's view caste is an organic system from which the element of competition has been rigorously excluded. This is corroborated by Bailey, who also writes that in the traditional system, castes do not compete with one another as blocks (Bailey 1963). Leach focusses on the 'recent' development of conflict between the landlords and agricultural labourers Kumbapettai village in Tanjore, described by Gough as a consequence of the transformation of landless labourer castes into a working class. Here, Leach is arbitrarily imputing

Fig. 3

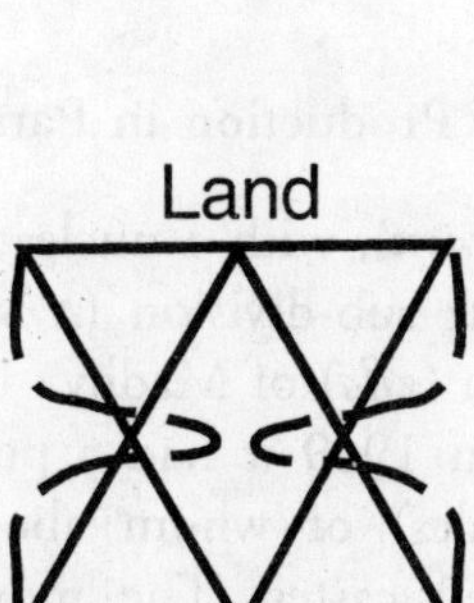

Fig. 4

historical causation to a feature (the existence of a large working class stratum) which is systemic.

In our formal model we suggest that in the Indian case, land and labour are polarised. The scaffolding of the typically Indian interface between caste and class is provided by the inverse relationship between land and labour (Fig. 4: p. 99).

If we view the system of social stratification in the above perspective, i.e., the perspective of agrarian structure, the numerically large classes at the top and bottom find their place in relation to the key variables of land and labour, while the numerically small class of non-agrarian specialists finds a place in the middle of the system. The following analysis is an attempt to penetrate the underlying structure of the rural class situation in India and, at the same time, assign to the overt structure of ritual reciprocities, their functional role in maintaining some kind of on-going equilibrium.

Some of the results of a field-project undertaken by me from 1969 to 1972 on 'status and power in the eastern Bundelkhand region of northern Madhya Pradesh, with special reference to economic networks and social change' are useful here. The following is an analysis of the relations of production between individuals, castes and classes in a village of Bundelkhand, Madhya Pradesh in north-central India.

Relations of Production in Parsania Village

Parsania is a village (*gaon*), with a nucleated settlement pattern, in the Laundi revenue sub-division (*tehsil*) of the Chhatarpur administrative division (*zila*) of Madhya Pradesh state (*rajya*) in the Indian Union.[1] In 1969 it had a population of 854 (472 males and 382 females) of whom about 30 per cent were members of scheduled castes. The most convenient way of getting to know about the village population was to ask how many households (*ghar*) of each of the different castes (*jati*) there were:

Table 1 Traditional Occupation

Brahmin	40	Priest
Bania	2	Trader
Ahir	2	Cattle-keeper
Gadariya	4	Shepherd
Sonar	1	Goldsmith
Lohar	2	Blacksmith
Barhai	2	Carpenter
Darzi	1	Tailor
Dhimar	5	Water-carrier
Kachi	21	Gardener
Kori	19	Weaver
Nai	2	Barber
Dhobi	3	Washerman
Kumhar	6	Potter
Chamar	40	Cobbler
Basor	6	Sweeper, midwife, basket-maker
Bahna	4	Cotton-carder
	160	

The homesteads of each large caste were clustered together.

Agricultural Cycle and Economic Classes

The villagers recognised four varieties of fields for agricultural operations.

Mota Thick, black soil for winter crops (*rabi*); wheat, gram, linseed.

Seench Soil irrigated by wells.

Bandhi Tank irrigated soil.

Har Grazing land; also land for cultivation alloted to the Scheduled Castes some eight years ago.

On the basis of their economic condition, village households were divided into those of *bhale log* (the gentry), *khate-pite log* ('all right' people) and *garib log* (poor). Lest it be thought that this classification emphasised consumption, I must immediately point out that it was intrinsically related to production. People viewed the annual agricultural cycle in relation to food grain—both for eating and sowing. The months according to the Hindu calendar are as follows:

Kharif	Chait	March-April	*Kharif* crops, dependant on dry cultivation are by definition inferior; labour inputs are small and soil-fertlity need not be high.
	Baisakh	April-May	
	Jeth	May-June	
	Asarh	June-July	
	Sawan	July-August	
	Bhadon	Aug-Sept.	
	Kuar	Sept.-Oct.	
	Kartik	Oct.-Nov.	
	Aghan	Nov.-Dec.	
Rabi	Pus	Dec.-Jan.	*Rabi* crops depend on wet cultivation and are superior; labour inputs are more; and fertility of land is decisive. Fertilisers are used. There is invariably a proportion of these crops devoted to growing inferior qualities, e.g, *jundi.* The cultivation of these crops is intended to feed labourers and inferior share-croppers.
	Magh	Jan.-Feb.	
	Phagun	Feb.-March	

There is, however, an important classification of this cycle from the point of view of the peasant (*kisan*) according to the 'discharge from the grain store' for sowing (*buwai*) or eating (*khawai*). Thus, from the point of view of the rich peasant, Asarh to Kuwar is *khawai;* Kuar to Agahan is *buwai;* and Agahan to Chait is *khawai*. This asymmetrical classification also puts into relief the fact that food grains should be viewed as values in commodity production and for the market.

The asymmetry is endemic. Such poor people who have their own land do not grow superior crops, but only inferior subsistence crops. If they have any surplus left from their bonded labour[2] it can be deployed only in producing subsistence crops with quick returns. This is one way of understanding the meaning of the common statement that 75 per cent of the 'good land' is in the hands of *bhale log*. According to whether the labour applied on land is free or unfree, we may classify the peasant population of Parsania into two classes corresponding to the categories, *bhale log* and *garib log*, with an intermediate category, as yet unformed into a class of middle peasants, of *khate-pite log*. The class of *bhale log* or rich peasants consists, in Parsania, exclusively of leading Brahmin families. The labour of rich peasants is maximally free in contrast to the maximal bondage of the labour of *garib log*. As I said before, besides cultivating their own inferior plots, they work as labourers on the fields of rich peasants. The majority of *garib log* are Chamars, but also include Dhimar, Kachi, Kori and Gadariya (see Table 1).

The Vocabulary for 'Masters'

The term *kisan* has an ambiguous connotation. It is the general north Indian term for 'peasant'. Depending on the context, the term is used to designate someone who tills the land, or someone who has his land cultivated. Alternatively the term *kisan* is confined to the families of rich peasants or middle peasants. The first usage includes most of the families of *bhale log, khate pite log* and *garib log*, with the exception only of those caste specialists, e.g., the untouchable Basor, who are neither cultivators nor tillers. This general usage of the term *kisan* has received greater currency since the legal abolition of all forms of tenancy and forced labour (*begar*) and the allotment (again *de jure*) of plots of unfertile land to the previously landless (e.g., a large number of Chamar families). The second, more restricted usage, relates to caste specialists. But whereas in the former case, the generalisation of the term is directly correlated with the legal abolition of *begar* and government grant of land leases to the previously 'landless', in the latter the *kisan* are only those well-to-do cultivators who are dominant co-sharers of land produce. Only the restricted usage is traditional. It belongs in the same series as *kisani,* the term used in Parsania village and throughout Bundelkhand for the hereditary master-servant relationship between families of cultivators and families of caste specialists. As I shall show later, the ritual of sowing in Parsania confounds the distinction between the two usages, both for the participants and the observer-analyst. Unless the analyst approaches agrarian production relations from the viewpoint of labour freedom and bondage, an objective study of ritual ideology among peasants may prove difficult.[3]

Classes of Cultivators and Servants

The following sketch of production relations is based on a rich peasant's account of the organisation of the annual agricultural cycle. We would do well to bear in mind that his total action in commodity production has two functions: providing subsistence and obtaining marketable surplus. I have deliberately omitted any reference to rights in land. There is a wide discrepancy between the legal and administrative definitions of these rights and how they are exercised in the village. The role of 'sea-lawyers' (Cohn 1965: 106-107) brings the two definitions together in the context of disputes, which I do not examine here.

Three crucial terms denotative of production relations should be noted.

I. *hissedar* or *sonjhdar* (co-sharer);
II. *harwaha* or *majdur* (ploughman-labourer);
III. *naukar* or *kam karne wala* (caste-specialist).

I. The co-sharing arrangement entered into by a rich peasant (*X*) with a poor cultivator (*Y*) takes three forms:

		X provides	*Y* provides	*Share of the produce*
(i)	*adhiya or bantai*	Plough, bullocks, implements, ½ labour	Land, well, and seed, ½ labour	*X* ½

		X provides	*Y* provides	*Share of the produce*
(ii)	*ji-kata ka sonjhiya or lak sonjhiya*	Implements, land and seed	Full labour + plough and bullocks	*Y* gets ¼ per plough
(iii)	*niyari*	—do—	Casual labour (i) for preparing post-irrigation land before winter sowing (ii) *danya* (preparing land) post-harvest.	*Y* gets one-third

II. The harwaha arrangement takes two forms:

(a) per diem payment of about Rs.3.00 or equivalent inferior crop; or

(b) *barhi* arrangement of grain-payment whereby the distinction from the point of view of the inferior partner, Y, between I (ii) and (iii) and II (b) is obliterated.

There is an institutional device called *barhi*, whereby the rich peasant by advancing crop-loans at usurious rates of interest is able to monopolise on the one hand the commodity production on the best land, and on the other, keep the productive labour of the village population under his servitude.

Grains are loaned under this arrangement at 25 per cent interest per annum (June to June), the rate of interest increasing on non-payment each year. Thus, if a man borrows one maund (40 seers or 8 paili) of wheat for sowing in November and continues to borrow throughout the year till June of the next year (when accounts are rendered) to the tune of one maund more, the amount borrowed will be 2 maunds plus interest at 25 per cent (*sawaya*), i.e., 2 mounds and 20 seers (or 2 maunds 4 paili). Normally, the loan arrangement is from June to June and includes the borrowing both of *kharif* and *rabi* crops for sowing and eating. The rate of increase of interest is such that for 3 consecutive years without repayment the interest doubles the amount originally borrowed. The borrower then has to repay in grain, cash, and labour over a long period. Even then he may not be able to clear the debt. At least 20 per cent of *garib log* in Parsania are debtors under *barhi* to the leading family of rich peasants in Parsania. The inferior crop-sharers as well as the ploughmen-labourers are all *kisan* (in the general sense) and distributed throughout the caste hierarchy. Nevertheless, a majority of them belong to non-dominant, non-specialised castes like the Kori and Kachi, and most are Chamar. The point is that the actual produce from the land is expropriated not only by rich peasants as organisers of commodity production but also by the corn-dealer and the village *bania*, directly in relation to the market and, indirectly, with regard to the organisation of production, as money-lenders, insisting that cash loans be repaid with interest in kind. In this sense, and in terms of the strong market nexus, (exclusively for the *bania*, and partly for the rich peasants), there exists a special commonality of interests (horizontal) between the rich peasants and the bania.

III. I have not yet brought into the picture, a third crucial term in production relations, namely, the *naukar* or *kam karne wala*. This category, comprising the caste specialists, stands in a reciprocal relationship to the *kisan*. The relations of production constitute the nexus of this reciprocity. This is seen most clearly in the *sudin* ritual that is performed in June, at the beginning of the annual agricultural cycle. When the *adra* star is sighted, the ritual of *sudin* is held. This ritual is a clear dramatisation of the categories of the relations of production. The substance of the ritual is the distribution of boiled wheat or *jowar* (*kohri*) by teams of rich peasants and their respective co-sharers for the year, to the *harwahe* and *naukar* (those mentioned were blacksmith, carpenter, washerman and barber) of each team. (The way, it was put to me, only those *harwahe* and *naukar* who have already agreed to work for a particular *kisan* that year, would accept *kohri*). While this is the individualising aspect of the ritual, the collective aspect—as a collective ritual of *kisani*—is underscored by the worship of wood, earth, houses and agricultural implements. These are showered with *kohri* and turmeric rice (yellow and white). Auspicious marks (*tilak*) are applied to agricultural implements.

The kisan propitiates the Gods praying that '*Bhagwan hamen raja aur praja se urin kare*' (May God enable us repay our debts to the *raja* [the King] and the *praja* [subjects].)

This ritual makes it clear that the category 'kisan' has a dual orientation: to the king and to his subjects. Its reciprocity in each direction is mediated by the other. Thus we may not understand the debt it (the collectivity 'kisan') owes, and feels constrained to repay the king, without taking into account the assimilation of this collectivity with the king's subjects (*praja*; here the revenue-payers). On the other hand, the debt it owes to its own subjects (*praja*; here the caste specialists) may not be understood without its assimilation with the king. This is an aspect of the ideological superstructure of peasants, the higher unity of which Marx was aware in his unfinished notes on the Asiatic mode of production (cf. Godelier 1965).

That the endemic asymmetry of the relations of production in this mode is overlaid by an ideological superstructure of reciprocities which obscures the contradictions between classes, is perfectly illustrated by the case at hand. What we know as *jajmani* elsewhere, is called *kisani* in Parsania and throughout Bundelkhand. Furthermore, overt linguistic usage is contradictory. As we have seen, those who are called *naukar* or *kam karne wale* in one context are called the *praja* in another context (ritual), and *bhai* ('brother', in opposition to the non-caste specialists and non-kisan villagers), in yet another context without the consciousness of this contradiction becoming apparent to the speakers.

The Vocabulary for Servants

All the contexts referred to pertain to the division of labour in the village. The first context is the most secular, in the sense that in its general usage, the category *naukar* or *kam karne wale* includes several non-caste specialists: the *harwahe*, other day-labourers, servants of all description. The usage *praja*, for servants, always implies a context defined by religious ideology. For example, a man of the oil presser caste in the neighbouring village of Bigpur was accused of having neglected his blind mother who, as a result, drowned herself in the village well. His caste council (*jati panchayat*) held him guilty of matricide. At the same time, the circumstance of her drowning in the village well from which all clean castes draw water caused pollution. As a result, caste-servants withdrew their services to the oil-presser. To counter the pollution of the well, the oil-presser was fined by the caste council elders and had to pay for an expiatory feast. At the same time he was beholden to the village council elders for ensuring the resumption of services to him by caste-specialists. In this case the elders were brahmins of Parsania (since Bigpur falls under the jurisdiction of Parsania village council). The oil-presser appealed with folded hands, to the elders of Parsania council saying: '*Malik praja roki gai hai*': 'My Lords, the *praja* [praja's services] have been discontinued'. This is an example of the vocabulary of 'brothers' being extended to servants. In this usage, the selection from the whole range of servants is further restricted. All non-caste specialists and unclean non-*kisan* villagers are excluded and it stands in perfect reciprocal relationship to the term, kisan.

Discussion

With the end of this demonstration, we now have only to relate our findings to the theoretical propositions concerning the study of Indian village communities advanced by Dumont (1966), and to go beyond. To deal with Dumont's objections to Maine first; I think Maine does not deserve the short shrift he gets from Dumont. Dumont has criticised Maine for the idealisation inherent in his understanding of the village community. This criticism may be more appropriately levelled against the more naive interpreters of Maine like some of the 'nationalist' post-independence writers who merged the 'political community' and 'dominant co-sharers' sense of 'brotherhood' to justify their own ideal representation of the village as a democratic organisation. The substance of Dumont's criticism of Maine is two-fold: first, that Maine confused the term 'brotherhood' with the village population at large, and secondly, he generalised from the 'democratic type' of village community, neglecting the more common aristocratic or simple type. Here Dumont follows Baden-Powell, whose several works on the land revenue system of British India had superseded Maine's writing on the village community. But Dumont fails to consider the inadequacies of Baden-Powell's typology (for a critique, cf. Fox 1971) and his misrepresentation of 'brotherhood'. Above all, Dumont omits Maine's treatment of the wider economic forces which is crucial to the latter's argument on stratification within the ill-defined 'brotherhood'. Maine was certainly inclined to confuse the idiom for the reality and remained inconclusive about the connotation of 'brotherhood'. However, my analysis has shown that this confusion is inherent in the overt forms of the 'master-servant' vocabulary in the villages of North India. Maine may only be criticised for not having resolved the confusion through his own analysis. But what direction might this analysis take? Dumont's conclusion:

> ...to be understood, the constitution of the village had to be put in relation to caste on the one hand, and to political power or traditional kingship on the other (1966:85).

points to a reductionist analysis: the reduction of all differences between the strata in the village community to ritual reciprocities; viz; those characterising *jajmani* and religious gifts. Our own analysis, on the other hand, focusses on the *kisan* rather than the *jati* structure and suggests that relations of ritual reciprocity form a part—perhaps, ideologically, the over-determining part—but do not in any sense constitute the whole of the relations of production between the agrarian classes. This conclusion is elaborated in what follows.

'The Indian Village Community': Division of Labour in the Peasantry

Dumont regards the *jajmani* complex as the ideological epitome of the division of labour in the Indian village. He writes:

> The division of labour in the Indian village is not strictly speaking

an economic fact; it is a 'holistic' (and, hence, largely religious) fact (Dumont 1967:34).

The meaning attached to religious holism is Hegelian. It is interesting that Hegel himself alluded to the paradox of dependence between the master and the servant. In this dialectic mode there was no resolution of the paradox, only its endless perpetuation. An exact analogy of this epistemological postulate is present in Dumont's global model of hierarchy.

Maine and Baden-Powell

Dumont discusses empirical facts in their structural relations to (dominant) hierarchical ideology; the relevant example for our present purpose is his critique of Sir Henry Maine's writings on the Indian village community (Dumont 1996). Maine characterised the socio-economic organisation of the Indian peasantry as a village community. The following passages from his book, *Village Communities in the East and West* (1871) summarise his main ideas on the subject.

> The village community is in India itself the source of a land-law which, in bulk at all events, may be not unfavourably compared with the real-property law of England. This law defines the relations to one another of the various sections of the group, and of the group itself to the Government, to other village communities, and to certain persons who claim rights over it (p. 18).
>
> ...[Though] there are strong general resemblances between the Indian village communities wherever they are found in anything like completeness, they prove on inspection to be not simple but composite bodies, including a number of classes with various rights and claims (p. 123).
>
> ...They [the Indian cultivating groups], in fact, include a nearly complete establishment of occupations and trade for enabling them to continue their collective life without assistance from any person or body external to them. Besides the Headman or council exercising quasi-judicial, quasi-legislative, power, they contain a village police, now recognised and paid in several provinces by the British Government. They include several families of hereditary traders: the Blacksmith, the Harness-maker, the Shoemaker. The

Brahmin is also found for the performance of ceremonies, and even the Dancing Girl.... There is invariably a Village Accountant.... But the person practicing any one of these hereditary employments is really a servant of the community as well as one of its component members. He is sometimes paid only an allowance of grain, more generally by the allotment to his family of a piece of cultivated land in hereditary possession (pp. 125-26).

The principal criticism I would make of Maine is not that he showed no understanding of castes but that he was not primarily interested in caste ideology though he showed interest in 'agricultural traditions'. He comments on the existence of named castes in the villages, but in passing (p. 175), or to minimise the role of caste divisions for understanding the organisation of the peasantry. It is true that he showed no understanding of the *jajmani* complex; even in the quotation above he fused the police and judicial functionaries with other functionaries. The source of this misunderstanding is to be traced to *Ancient Law* (Maine 1861) which is an exercise in old-fashioned social evolutionism.(Though a critical study of even that work is not to be discarded out-of-hand if one is trying to understand, comparatively, the characteristics of religious feudalism.) More to the point in the present context, is the value of Maine's characterisation of the village community for understanding the *kisan* structure that I have analysed in a village of a backward region of central India. Maine raises the question of the 'village community' and 'brotherhood' twice in his book:

> ...the customary rules securing the interdependence and mutual responsibility of an Indian village community, or the various subordinate groups which it may be shown to include, and the modes of speech in use among them, which are said to fluctuate between language implying an hereditary brotherhood, and language implying a voluntary association, appear to be worthy of careful examination (p. 117).
>
> The end for which it [the village community] exists is the tillage of the soil, and it contains within itself the means of following its occupation without help from outside. The brotherhood, besides the cultivating families [read *kisan*] who form the major part of the

> group comprises families [read *praja* and *bhai*] which furnish the little society with articles of use and comfort (p. 175).

Maine's notion of brotherhood in the village community can be explicated with reference to the terms added by me in parenthesis. As I have shown in my village ethnography, even the linguistic indicator, *bhai* (brother) is present in the ritual context of interaction between the rich peasants (*kisan*) and caste specialists (*praja*).

In all subsequent writings on the Indian village community, Baden-Powell's works completely superseded Maine's book. Baden-Powell was a pragmatist and utilitarian thinker. More than that he was a revenue administrator. He lacked Maine's intellectual curiosity. His classification of the land revenue systems of British India is an example of butterfly-collection. In the opening chapter of his book , *Indian Village Community* (1896) Baden-Powell sought to demolish Maine. He added the gloss 'tenant' to Maine's 'inferiors and dependents', introduced the terms 'tenant, farm-labourer, low caste menial', then went on to write:

> ... I am not aware that in any case tenants form part of the 'brotherhood', or that they can be represented as occupying a grade in any sort of hierarchy formed by the 'brotherhood'. The proprietors alone have a voice in the management. Tenants, even when they are so privileged a class as to pay no rent beyond the Government dues, usually pay a nominal fee... for their house site... Still less are the artisans and menial parts of the 'brotherhood' in any degree whatever: they are always of different (usually lower) caste. Indeed the idea that, e.g., a body of proud Rajput co-sharers would acknowledge their cultivating tenants, and *a fortiori* the potter, the carpenter, or the chamar, as part of their brotherhood, only in a lower degree, is something quite grotesque (p. 26).

Because of his official interest in defining jural rights in land held by corporate bodies, Baden-Powell translated Maine's notion of brotherhood in substantive terms. It is ironical, indeed, that Maine who has been compared unfavorably with Baden-Powell for his relative lack of practical experience of rural life in India, showed much more sensitivity to modes of speech, constituting the initial context in which he placed 'brotherhood'. Furthermore, nowhere in his book does Maine consider the Chamar as forming part of the brotherhood, which specification must be considered a product of Baden-Powell's own mind. It is an apt illustration of his taking undue advantage of the interconnections between the notions of brotherhood and village community left vague in Maine's own writing.

Dumont's Critique of Maine

Maine's lumping of together the brotherhood and the village community is only a small part of Dumont's critique. One of his principal criticisms is that Maine generalises from the democratic type of village community to the virtual neglect of the simple or aristocratic type. Resting his case primarily on Baden-Powell's typology, Dumont claims the latter type of village community to have been far more common in pre-British and early British India. Dumont uncritically accepts the testimony of Maine's contemporary, Campbell, in whose opinion 'property in the soil' in the simple or aristocratic type of village community was of the lowest description, amounting to little more than a very strong tenant-right. The democratic communities, by contrast, had a much stronger form of property, 'rent' being paid by the landlords to some government and by inferior holders to superior holders.

Unlike Maine, Dumont fails to appreciate the following:

(a) that the question of defining 'tenant' was a difficult one Dumont accepts Campbell's theory (Campbell 1852) that tenants were former superior holders who had been displaced by conquest by a new superior group, and

(b) the question whether what was paid by the village communities to the governmental power was revenue or rent which remains contentious even to this day. (Elsewhere Dumont (1967) himself seems inclined to regard this payment as revenue; a sixth of the cultivator's produce being the ruler's traditional share or *bhag*.)

Maine clearly saw both these difficulties. The idea of competitive rents, he wrote, was alien to village communities in India. Yet he recognised the limited operation of market forces in relation to land and its produce. Hence he mentions customary rents and prices in addition to revenue which idea, (besides being a useful support for his view of the Indian village as primitive in an evolutionary sense), enabled him to account for taxes, excise-rates, payment of interest on loans etc...i.e., monetary transactions entering the wider economic and political networks of village communities. The point here is that Maine proceeded in the right direction. He never speaks of tenants, either to designate landlords who were payees to the government or to characterise inferior and dependent classes and sub-classes of cultivators within the village community. One may confidently add that the nature of proprietary rights in land could not be grasped without an analysis of the relations of production expressed in native institutions and affected by market forces. Historical evidence from early nineteenth century British India and from territories of native states to a considerably later period suggests that the wider economic and political forces affected these relations unilaterally. In other words, the agricultural surplus derived from the village and converted into money was not fed back into the process of agricultural production (cf. Barrington Moore 1969; Maddison1971 etc.). This dominant economic structure cut across the typology, 'aristocratic or simple' and 'democratic'.

The explanation of Dumont's uncritical acceptance of Baden-Powell's and Campbell's typology and his allergy to the concept of economic forces affecting the village community, is furnished by the second prong of his attack on Maine:

> ...to be understood, the constitution of the village had to be put in relation to caste on the one hand, and to political power or traditional kingship on the other (Dumont 1966:75).

It is necessary to underline once again that in his critique of Maine, Dumont nowhere mentions his treatment of economic factors. At first sight this is a surprising omission, since Maine was led to consider precisely these factors to account for the social stratification and hierarchy of the brotherhood. But this is made comprehensible by the terms of Dumont's alternative theory: namely, the hierarchy theory of the Indian caste system. As I shall argue later, this theory—accepting, and indeed rigidifying, as ideological postulate, the *jajmani* complex—has had the potential of short-circuiting all discussion of economic factors in considering division of labour amongst the Indian peasantry. We first encounter this in a footnote to Dumont's paper on Maine in his inconclusive observation that the existence of strata within the brotherhood is a matter either of hierarchy or of dominance (ibid:87). Dumont spells out his entire theory in *Homo Hierarchicus* (1970). In terms of this theory, there is, in Indian society, the hierarchical encompassment of power or dominance by the encompassing status ideology. In this holistic religious ideology, economic and political power exist undifferentiated as dominance. Moreover, since for Dumont, the conscious ideology itself provides the framework for explanation or understanding, the conclusion is inevitable that his explanation of social strata in the brotherhood, (either the internal stratification of landholders and cultivators or of the village population at large), would be the existence of ritual reciprocities between castes. This is precisely the case. As a result, economic factors are wiped away never to reappear.

The Notion of 'Hierarchic Reciprocity' and Division of Labour

A few words should be said about the classification of ritual reciprocities in the *jajmani* complex, and the generalisation of this classification to the division of labour in the Indian peasantry. Dumont's position in this respect is unequivocal, and has progressively hardened. The structure he discovers in the division of labour in the village communities is one of 'hierarchic reciprocity' (Dumont and Pocock 1957:31). About Wiser's celebrated depiction of the jajmani system, Dumont and Pocock remark:

> This idea of a harmonious system of reciprocal service, despite its evident romanticism, has stuck, although any field worker has only to think of his proud landowning peasantry to realise that the more absolute the dominance, the less is reciprocity recognised... Thus, in Wiser's chart we are told that the Brahmin and related castes are served by all and also serve the first 19 castes of the village. In point of fact... this is not so. From Wiser's figures we can see that in Karimpur only five of the 41 Brahmin families functioned as priests while the remainder were large and small landowners served by others and recognising no obligation to serve themselves (ibid:30).

Their explanation of Wiser's romanticism in the face of the actual unilateral reciprocity received by the 'proud landowning peasantry' (an echo of Baden-Powell?) is as follows:

> In this village the dominant caste was also the Brahmin caste and, as so frequently happens when the one caste also stands in the two distinct structural positions, the two are confused in analysis.

The two distinct structural positions are those of landownership and priesthood, or, dominance and ritual status. However, the unit to which both these attributes are attached is the same—caste. Dumont and Pocock do not ask the next logical question, viz., how does this common unit, (not merely a participant-category but an observer and analysts' category as well), operate in relation to landownership? More precisely, they differentiate on the basis of Wiser's data between brahmin families which do, and do not perform religious services in the village. However they do not differentiate either the families of brahmin caste or the village population as a whole in respect of landownership. In Pocock's detailed ethnography of a region of Gujarat the same lack of concern regarding landownership persists, and in respect of this important variable concerning Patidar dominance he presents us with a non-sequiter, namely, the premise of a congruence between social and economic graduality in the village population (Pocock 1972; Jain 1973). However, Dube who is directly concerned with the distribution of power in rural society finds caste as a unit to be of no explanatory value in the description and analysis of rural factionalism (Dube 1968; cf. also McCall 1971 for an analysis of Mayer's ethnography of 'allied castes' in Ramkheri). Dumont brings about a congruence between caste as the unit of both ritual status and dominance (e.g., landownership) by introducing the notion of hierarchic reciprocity; more precisely, by characterising or typifying the dominant caste as the *jajman* par excellence.[4]

In their early joint writing referred to above, Dumont and Pocock felt the need for 'distinguishing relationships based upon ritual beliefs from those which are purely economic' (p. 32), but the distinction they suggested was within the set of *jajmani* relationships themselves: 'those based upon purity and impurity beliefs from relationships of an economic nature' (p. 31). The 'positions' mentioned in the former category are the bhangi, the brahmin, the barber, the water-bearer and the washerman; those mentioned in the latter category are the goldsmith, the florist, the carpenter, and the potter. Pocock in his'Notes on Jajmani Relationships' went on to suggest a third category comprising 'landholding and laboring castes' in jajmani or jajmani-type relationships (Pocock 1962:94) though still maintaining that the ideology of caste governs all persons and groups involved in these relationships. However, even this slight departure in the direction of the economic context of village division of labour[5] was not in keeping with the opposition between 'holistic' versus the 'individualistic' orientations in Dumont's global model of hierarchy. He writes:

> ...[One] should keep in mind the too-neglected observation of Weber in his inventory of the forms of division of labour, recalling, in opposition to the orientation to the individual profit characteristic of what is strictly called 'economics', the holistic orientation of the system (sic.). In particular, in view of this orientation, it is not of fundamental interest to try and distinguish precisely between religious and economic aspects, i.e., presumably between holistic and individualistic aspects.

The Study of Peasantry and the Lack of a Model of Market Forces

It will not be wholly true to say that all social anthropologists have been equally insensitive to the economic factors in studying the division of labour in Indian villages. Most discussions of *jajmani* take into account the demographic changes, variations in the supply and demand of goods and services by various specialists, and the processes of migration caused by these variations. However, the interest of the analysts remains focussed on occupational specialisation in the village population derived from the caste status of individuals and families. The position of the merchant or the trader is that of the 'imps' of the hierarchy; unfortunately, I cannot, here entertain that subject. The analytical vocabulary adopted for the study of the peasantry derives from this focus and comprises a few sets of terms: the dominant caste (variations: 'Peasant Caste' in Epstein; 'Farmer Caste'in Mayer); the jajmani system of relationships; village 'holism; hierarchic reciprocity. Whenever indigenous vocabulary is reported, e.g., *jajman-kamin*, *purjan*, *hali*, *majur*, *bhagia*, etc. to denote classes of masters and servants in the village community, the classificatory grid either of the caste system or of the administrative and revenue typology is imposed to order relationships designated by these terms. The administrative and revenue typology receives more attention from those social anthropologists who undertake class analysis or studies of social change. A good example is Andre Beteille's study of social stratification in Sripuram village of Tanjore district in which the categories 'landowner', 'tenant' and 'agricultural labourer' are used to designate classes in an otherwise caste-cum-party political analysis of social change. Like Bailey and Cohn, Beteille sets a seemingly arbitrary historical base-line (nearly 150 years ago) for the study of market forces: 'the time since land entered market'. In fact, it can be shown that for practical reasons these social anthropologists have determined their base-line in the same fashion as would administrative historians, i.e., since the time that land-records began to be maintained by British revenue officials and their subordinates. The question does, however, arise as to whether or not we would be correct in accepting the classification of the peasantry *determined* in official records by the constraints of a free market model. That the regulations emanating from this model were enforced by conscientious administrators cannot be denied, but questions of immense importance in the study of the peasantry are: to what extent and to whose advantage? More specifically, in relation to official definitions of such categories as landowners, tenants, and agricultural labourers, how are we to translate these terms as operational concepts in a study of agrarian production relations at the village level? No serious reader of the massive official literature dealing with the Indian village in the nineteenth century would doubt that the enforcement of regulations affected the higher echelons of society while leaving the lower ones to the devices of the former. An instance of the analytical vacuity of this literature from our point of view is the official typification of the peasantry as proprietors, sub-proprietors and 'others' without the crucial notions of property and ownership being ever explained. Gradually, it seems that the peasantry as a whole, both in sociological and in official literature, came to be viewed as being synonymous with *kisan* plus the *jajmani* complex while the basic anthropological problems of translation at the village level remained unsolved.

Faced with the plethora of official definitions and classifications, modern historians have begun to encounter difficulties precisely in the same area of information and conceptualisation that Maine had in 1875 (cf. Frykenberg 1969):

> Since I have had any knowledge of India, nothing seemed to me more remarkable than the degree to which the ideas of the Indian government, and consequently, the fortunes of the Indian population, have been affected by what I regard as questions of words, questions, namely, as to words descriptive of Western phenomena which can be properly used of Eastern facts and institutions (Maine, cited in Dumont 1965:95).

Without prejudice to Maine's (or Dumont's) own

predilections towards the terms of a global comparison (western and eastern; individualistic and holistic) we may, nevertheless, try finally to chart the different directions which their analyses take. Maine was specifically anti-Marx, (on the point of private property; 1871:229-230), saw a possible convergence between his views and those of Marx, (on the point of the village community), and reacted strongly to any prospect of an identity between his views and those of Marx. Yet, separated as both Marx and Maine are from us now by more than a century, we must make an effort to study the convergence of their ideas. One topic suggests itself: a model of market forces in relation to nineteenth century village communities in India, whether we choose to call it a specific pre-capitalistic Mode of Production, one mediated by the ideological and institutional constraints of reproduction, or a theory of customary rents and prices. The task needs collaboration between social anthropologists and economic historians.

The Religious Ideology of the Gift and the Explanation of Land Ownership in Kerala

On the anthropologists' special contribution to the study of peasantry past and present, I would differ from Dumont in one major respect. His notion of hierarchic reciprocity typifying the division of labour in the Indian peasantry cannot, at one and the same time, be both the dominant religious ideology and the intellectual instrument for explaining the objective function of that ideology. This is a crucial point bearing on the interpretation of social stratification in rural India by explicating the meaning of native categories in the context of usage. A specific example, namely, Dumont's interpretation of the rights in land in Kerala may help to clarify our difference of approach. There, in Dumont's terms, is no *dominant caste* but *dominance*.[6] The relation of dominance to land is not that of 'property'. The individual agent (the holder of rights in land produce) is not a substance but a term in a relation, minimally dyadic. Thus the functional equivalent of the concept 'property' (as understood in individualistic societies), has here to be sought in 'ownership', embedded in a holistic formula:

> ...the rights in land in Kerala, more exactly Malabar, were...spilt between an upper right or *janmam*, 'birthright', and a lower right or *kanam*, 'right by gift',

which was acquired or maintained by periodically giving *kanam* to the upper rightholder. (This complementarity does not take into account the inferior lessees). The holders of kanam and janmam shared between themselves some two-thirds of the produce of the land leased to others. They may be taken together as enjoying something like ownership, excluding the right to alienation (Dumont 1965:97). It is surprising that Dumont does not refer to Miller's earlier article (Miller 1956) specifying the nature of the *janmi-kanakkaran* relationship:

> the relationship... was less a contractual relationship between landlord and tenant than an incident of the respective status of each in relation to land.

While Dumont does not at all specify the status of these masters in relation to the servants, Miller goes on to say:

> [Somewhat] similarly, the various servicing castes, such as washermen, owed their obligations first to the village as a whole, and only derivatively to a particular caste, subcaste, or family.

While this cryptic comment itself bristles with obscurities (what, for instance, is the meaning of 'somewhat similarly', or 'derivatively' etc.), one crucial omission in both Miller and Dumont is noteworthy. The servants of the village as a whole do not for them include the large number of manual labourers, agreistic serfs (Kumar 1962:337-63). My basic point, then, is that the discussion by social anthropologists of the relationship between population and land in the villages of Kerala has left out the most significant component in the treatment of peasantry: the productive labour of men and women in the fields! Both Dumont and Miller are sensitive to native linguistic categories: Dumont provides translations of both '*janmam*' and '*kanam*'; Miller adduces a native linguistic usage, "*Desam avakasam*" (Miller's translation 'a privilege in the land'), to explain the orientation to 'the village as a whole' of obligations of the caste specialists-(although only the washerman is specifically mentioned). Might it not be that they failed to press their enquiries into linguistic usages further to subsume manual labourers? This is possible but not very probable. In fact, Miller is the ethnographer in question and he does designate manual labourers by their caste (*jati*). But this definitely exhausts the extent of his interest in this category of 'servants'. (Kumar who turns to the works of social anthropologists and administrators to seek illumination precisely for this category of servants, hits her head against the wall of caste erected by them in common. However, she profits more by her own economic analysis of administrators' reports, than by the writings of anthropologists.)

The only explanation, by no means an original one, I can offer for the lack of penetration in anthropological discussions of manual labourers or agreistic serfs in the population of rural Malabar, is that they have seized upon the ubiquitous indigenous category 'jati' both to observe, and classify, the population into groups in their field research and to explain the structure of peasant society. I have already referred to the former procedure in Miller's account of manual labourers in Malabar. We may, in conclusion, note the continuity in Miller's and Dumont's procedures of explanation although the former is a structural-functionalist and the latter a structuralist in anthropological jargon. Both subscribe to the view that the conscious models, (native explanations), of the people being studied, should be taken into account in any explanation of the social structure of an alien society. An extra resource available to the anthropological analyst of literate societies like India, are the exegesis of indigenous and non-indigenous literati. As an analytical instrument, however, this resource is a double-edged sword. The notion of hierarchic reciprocity, exemplified by the structure of jajmani and the ideology of the gift, is one reproduction of this resource. In Miller's analysis this takes the form of a distinction between the spiritual authority of the brahmins and the temporal authority of the Samantama and the *janmi* Nayar. The resource itself is religious or ritual in its immanence. The question one asks is what is its function? Basically, it perpetuates ambiguity. We should be warned against its use as an instrument of scientific, objective, analysis if—as we have demonstrated both with reference to the small experiment on interrelations between classes engaged in agricultural production in Parsania, and concerning the role of manual labourers in Malabar—it serves to obscure rather than reveal contradictions between classes. In that case, as we have tried to do, the instrument itself becomes the first object of our analysis.

A more general lesson is that as we proceed to a new mode of analysing Indian peasantry, (for example the study of the *kisan* structure), we would do well to guard against the uncritical adoption of a native category as a category of analysis. Unless this caution is observed, we are likely to impose a single connotation on the category *kisan*: the rhetoric of the nationalist movement, for example, has sufficiently influenced the literati, some politicians and administrators in modern India so as to generate a popular, romantic view of the *kisan*. The whole history of caste or *jati* studies in peasant anthropology is a live illustration of the pitfalls we have to avoid.

Notes

1. Before 1948 the formal government was very different. Laundi tehail was a revenue sub-division of the native kingdom of Chhatarpur, ruled over by a scion of the Panwar Rajput ruling house. My account is based strictly on field-notes based on observations and conversations with villagers from July to December 1969.
2. I am using the term 'bonded labour' not only in its restricted legal meaning of 'debt bondage' but also to include those circumstances of poor cultivators where they may be debarred from tilling their own land because their labour has been monopolised by rich peasants. The latter are also the ones who enjoy the monopoly of the best land in the village.
3. Tambiah (1973) has shown in a study of Hindu representations,

'From Varna to Jati, through Mixed Unions', that the generation of a third class by the intermixture of two classes was the standard classificatory procedure of ancient codemakers. However, other rules of procedure (like *anuloma* and *pratiloma*) were added to the above rule so that eventually all classes so generated could be assigned to the poles of purity and impurity which remained distinct. The perception of this procedure is significant for understanding the status ideology of the Hindus. Is it an analytical instrument to determine the objective function of that ideology in society?

4. The generalisation: the congruence between 'social and economic graduality' (Pocock) and 'hierarchic reciprocity' (Dumont) receive support from Srinivas's vague generalisation emanating from his own view of caste: 'A large and powerful caste group can more easily be dominant if its position in the local hierarchy is not too low.' The vagueness of this generalisation is highlighted by numerous empirical exceptions, viz., the Nayar in Kerala, the Lodha in Bundelkhand villages, the Raj Gond etc., but we shall not here digress on that point.
5. I note here a refreshing change in that Pocock refers to Maine. Unfortunately he fails to pursue the matter far enough, especially as he confuses rent with price.
6. This, I believe, may be the correct interpretation of the position of the Nayars where they held *janmi* rights of hereditary headmanhips in the *desam*. Referring to the extreme status-fragmentation among the Nayar or Kerala (as also the Newar of Nepal), Dumont prefers to speak of 'populations' rather than caste groups: 'All these (the various status grades of Nayar, for example) are actually status groups, and one can look at the whole population as being divided into status groups which may be absolutely (or practically) endogamous at the one end, and exogamous at the other' (Dumont 1964:98).

CHAPTER VI

Status and Power in Bundelkhand: A Summing Up

Western sociologists and anthropologists have been attempting to understand Indian society for a long time. What interests them particularly about Indian society, as compared to other societies and cultures, is the idiom of high and low castes, and of untouchability. This emphasis on the hierarchical aspect of caste expressed through ritual and symbol dominates their thinking. It is not as though these scholars are ignorant of the occupational basis of the caste system. Nor do they ignore that aspect of caste organisation which is related to the status of caste within particular regions of India. In fact, if we keep in mind both these aspects—regional variation and the occupational basis of the caste system—then we get a perspective on the direction of present and past changes in Indian social structure. But most western sociologists have not paid any attention to this. I consider this a serious weakness, the implications of which shall be reviewed later. For example, Prof. N.K. Bose has pointed out (Bose 1959) that with the abolition of the Permanent Settlement in Bengal, the occupational basis of the caste system in the state became progressively weaker. In Bengal, along with the Brahmins, the Vaidyas and the Kayasthas were also included among the bhadralok class. Due to economic and political reasons the social status of the Kayastha caste is higher among the Bengalis, than in U.P., Bihar and other areas. Similarly, the social status of brahmins in Punjab and Gujarat is not considered as high as among the Kanyakubja brahmins of U.P. and the Sri Vaishnav and Smartha brahmins of Tamil Nadu. There have also been variations in the social status of Kanyakubja brahmins according to region and historical period. Those Kanyakubja brahmins who left the area of the Doab and settled in Bundelkhand are considered lower in status to the 'Antarvedi' Kanyakubja. Even today, in Chhatarpur district, men of the Kanyakubja caste have difficulty in finding marriageable younger women for themselves and, when they take spouses from the Doab region, they have to pay high dowries. Till recent times, the Kanyakubja brahmins solved this problem by the practice of marrying their daughters to the Jujhotia brahmins, settled for a long time in Bundelkhand. In traditional terms, the Kanyakubja brahmins have considered the Jujhotias to be of a lower status and according to the rules of hypergamy, the Jujhotias have been giving their daughters to the Kanyakubjas. But for about 30 years or so, having decided that they would abandon the idiom of high and low amongst themselves, the Jujhotia Mahasabha have stopped giving their daughters in marriage to Kanyakubja brahmins.

What light do these changing relationships, between Kanyakubja and Jujhotia brahmins in this area throw on the social dynamics in Chhatarpur? Before answering this question, let me first give a general introduction to certain aspects of social structure in Eastern Bundelkhand.

A Macro-profile of Social Structure in Eastern Bundelkhand

First of all, let us unravel the meaning behind the proposition that 'in Indian society castes are traditionally endogamous'. Not only among the Kanyakubja and Jujhotia brahmins but even in other communities, sub-castes, like the Banaphar Rajput, the Bundelkhandi Tamere, the Parwar Jains etc., are considered endogamous. But, when we look closely at their marital relationships, we find that marriage is not limited to their own group. As we have seen before, brahmin sub-castes such as the

Kanayakubja and Jujhotia, may appear endogamous in the light of similar sub-castes, but among themselves, they are divided on traditional grounds, into many endogamous sub-units, such as the Biswa among the Kanyakubja, the Pata among the Jujhotias, and the Kuri among the Rajputs. On the other hand, they have marital relationships with other sub-divisions (sub-castes or clans) like the Bundela, the Dhandhera and the Panwar Rajputs, the Kanyakubja and the Jujhotia brahmins, the Parwar and Golapurab Jains etc. However, if we examine the marital relationships within a region, it becomes clear that within this limit, their marital ideals are changeable. All over India, in order to avoid caste mixture, and to preserve traditional social status, appropriate marriages are sought to be brought about. About the Bundelkhandi Rajputs, Luard wrote (Luard 1909) that Dhandhere, Bundele and Panwar Rajputs are exogamous groups. But the group of these three castes is endogamous. Luard also said that two or three generations ago these Rajput groups intermarried with other Rajput houses also. It may be conjectured that this endogamous limit applied to commoners among Rajputs because Luard himself has written elsewhere (Luard 1928) that the last ruler of Chhatarpur, Bhawani Singh, who was a Panwar Rajput married the daughter of the Patiala Maharaja and made her his senior queen. This kind of flexibility in marriage rules and the difference between commoners and ruling houses with regard to marriages is found in every region of India. My intention in providing the example of the Chhatarpur ruling house is to remind fellow sociologists that caste rules do not apply equally to all classes within a caste. There have been classes in India right from early times and, in order to consolidate and expand their power, the ruling houses among the Hindus have kept politics above the rules of caste.

If the flexibility of marriage rules was a feature only of ruling houses, then, it would not have had much influence on an understanding of folk life in Bundelkhand as a whole. But I believe that during the Moghal and British periods, wherever there were small Hindu kingdoms, the ruling houses had a great deal of influence on the regional social structure and on norms in the region. Historians and sociologists agree that when fairly large areas of north India came under the rule of the Muslims and the British, these foreign rulers could not identify with the social organisation of rural areas. In other words, whereas on the one hand there was contact between the rural people and the foreign powers for purposes of revenue and maintenance of peace, on the other hand, the reins of religion and politics came fully into the hands of influential twice-born houses. In contrast to the masters in princely states, in the districts and provinces ruled by the British, the rural people had no higher power to complain to against the local zamindars and jagirdars. In the Hindu princely states, the peasants had to pay many such taxes which were related to the personal life of their rulers. Even today among all the princely states of Bundelkhand, the economic interdependence among the various castes of the villages is known as '*kisani*' rather than '*jajmani*'. Even the Basor, Chamar, Kumhar, Lohar, Barhai, Dhobi, Nai and Harwaha have their own *kisan*. They are paid for their labour both in cash and in kind and this remuneration is known as *kamnauti*. The rate of *kamnauti* is settled through negotiation between the *kisan* and their workers. During my research in Parsania village, Laundi Tehsil, Chhatarpur district, I encountered the language in which these relationships were expressed. According to William Wiser, in his book *The Hindu Jajmani System*, in a village called Karimpur near Kanpur, the masters are known as *jajman* and the workers as *kamin*. In Parsania village, on the other hand, the masters are known as *kisan* and the workers are known as *bhai* or *praja*. It is my guess that the people who, in the Doab region are called *kamin*, and *bhai* or *praja* in Bundelkhand, reflect two different social ideologies. In this milieu, the *kisan* is equated with *raja* i.e. the authority to whom revenue is payable. Even today, during the month of Asarh, (i.e., June-July) at the time of the sowing season, the *kisan* in Bundelkhand pray to God as follows '*Bhagwan hamen raja aur praja se urin kare*' (May God help us pay our debts to *raja* and *praja*).

The Context of the Village

In a social milieu where the village folk are intimately related to the authority of the ruling house, it is understandable that those who perform traditional duties are called *praja*. In the context of village life (*gaondari*) the term *praja* is used mostly in contexts where the caste or village panchayat is prosecuting somebody. For example, if a person is accused of matricide then it is said that the *praja* available to him at home will be stopped which means that the traditional workers will no longer provide their services to his household. As we have pointed out the same workers are ordinarily called '*bhai*'. In other words, we can say that the idiom of *kisani* in the village is dependent on the authority of the ruling house. And, in this particular respect, it seems that the economic and social relationships of the village are cast in an idiom of equality rather than inequality.

I have so far looked at the historical backdrop in which certain political and economic aspects are found in Eastern Bundelkhand. I shall now show how religious elements are involved in this picture. This is especially true of the period before 1948, in the state of Chhatarpur. As pointed out earlier, in the princely states of Bundelkhand, the houses of twice-born castes in the villages did not have the same authority of social disciplining as they had under foreign rule in British administered territories. At the same time, we have seen that the Kanyakubja brahmins of this region are considered to be of a lower status than the Kanyakubja of the Doab region. In this region, both the Kanyakubja and Jujhotia brahmins considered themselves the descendants of the same ancestors. Both these castes settled in Bundelkhand after migration from Kannauj.

Migration History as a Factor in Social Structure

The story about this migration, which I picked up from Parsania village, was that the ruler of Orchha, Jhujhar Singh, invited Kanyakubja brahmins to perform *yagya* at the death of his brother Hardaul. Thirteen brahmins accepted this invitation and were called Jujhotias. After that, three more brahmins came. They were also called Jujhotia. Thus the Jujhotias were divided into endogamous divisions of three and thirteen. The descendants of all these were known as Jujhotia brahmins. Those Kanyakubja brahmins who did not participate in this *yagya* but came later to this region in search of a living, became the ancestors of the Bundelkhandi Kanyakubjas. Thus, the status of the brahmins in this area is determined by the order of their migration. According to the Kanyakubjas, the Jujhotias are of a lower status because they are descendants of those Kanyakubjas who participated in a ritual celebrated by Jhujhar Singh to atone the death of his brother whom he had killed by poisoning. In any case, all these Jujhotias and the Kanyakubjas, are considered to be of a lower status for two reasons: first, because they left their original home and second, because they were attracted to the region by the allurement of the gift (*dan*) offered by the kings. Also noteworthy is that most probably, the Rajputs of this region were originally non-Hindu aboriginals who got their brahmin priests to legitimise their status as Kshatriyas by offering gifts to them. In this milieu, on the one hand, the brahmins, therefore, received royal patronage and on the other, drifted from their original religious ways towards folk religion, politics and *gurus* of different sects. Based on this, we can make three propositions about the social and religious status and influence of the brahmins in this area. Firstly, the brahmins of this area did not hold the highest authority in rural society. Secondly, in the religious sphere, the influence of the brahmins was mainly used to legitimise powerful victors such as the Kshatriyas. Nonetheless, although they legitimised the power of upstart conquerers, they, in turn, remained dependent on royal power for their own maintenance, with the result that the masses also looked upon them as 'dependent' agents. Thirdly, as a result of these tendencies, the religious ideals of the masses here were different from those of the Hindus in other parts of India. It would not be an exaggeration to say that their ideals were not influenced much by the Vedic or Sanatan Hindu religion. If these propositions have any truth, then perhaps they provide a key to understanding Bundelkhandi folk life.

Dominance of Indigenous Tradition: The Case of Rituals and Celebrations

When we look at the religious traditions and tendencies of village folk in Bundelkhand, the non-dominance of Vedic elements becomes quite apparent. It is true that the twice-born castes abide by Vedic rituals, yet even amongst them, family rituals and regional rituals are dominant, like the worship of Gond Baba, Thakur Baba, Bhim Devta, Hardaul Lala etc. These cults are indigenous to the history and mythology of Bundelkhand. There are many examples that suggest that even the brahmins of this area have been greatly influenced by these religious tendencies.

I was completely unfamiliar with the way in which the festival of Deepavali is celebrated in Bundelkhand villages during the month of Kartik. On the day after Deepavali, there is a tradition of '*maun charana*'. This tradition requires devotees to observe a two-day fast, while going in a procession through the sacred spots in the village in complete silence (*maun*). As they walk, the devotees, impersonate Lord Krishna's cows by symbolically grazing (*charana*). In the Parsania village, as we have seen, brahmins are the dominant caste. There are no Thakurs, and other high castes are in a minority. For this reason, most of the brahmins in Parsania regard *maun charana* as a lower caste celebration. The brahmins do not attend *maun charana*, nor do they dance the 'diwari'. In Parsania, this celebration is typical of the menfolk of the Kori, Chamar, Kumhar and Nai castes. Men of the Ahir and Gadaria castes dance with the Mauni ascetics, and the drummers are from the Basor caste. However, the brahmins of Parsania told me that in the villages on the east bank of the river Ken, and also in the villages adjacent to Laundi, the brahmins and Thakurs participate fully in *maun charana*. It would be interesting to analyse the symbolism of *maun charana* as it might throw some light on the cultural and social structure of Bundelkhand, but this is not possible within the current discussion. There is a belief that the devotees who have taken this vow (*vrata*) of *maun charana* should observe it for twelve years: it is believed that twelve years is the period of time that Lord Krishna grazed the cows. It is believed that by performing the *vrata* for this period the devotees earn great merit and go to heaven. This form of *bhakti* or devotion is celebrated irrespective of caste. Even in Parsania village, the brahmins have one role in this celebration. Before the start of *maun vrata* and at the end of this fast, the brahmin priest worships a calf brought by the devotees. The calf is then gifted to the brahmin priest.

I should also mention another custom of the original (Bhumia) inhabitants of the village. On the day after Deepavali, the four Bhumia families of the village arrange a *yatra* to the shrine of Pehalwan Singh Thakur which is located on the northern boundary of Parsania village. The main celebrant is Budhoo Gadaria who is believed to go into a trance *(bhava khelta hai)* and incarnate the spirit of Behnar Singh Thakur. In the language of Bundelkhand, he became the horse (*ghoda*) of Behnar Singh Thakur. Another Gadaria who went into a trance became the 'horse' of Gwal Baba. Similarly Sakhan Teli became the 'horse' of Pahalwan Singh Thakur. Others who participate in this *yatra* are Kasia Kori who was possessed by Devi and Chota Lohar who smoked marijuana. *(ganja)* with the other horses and was also involved in answering questions in the manner of an oracle. Through the medium of these horses, Thakur Gwal Baba answered questions on behalf of Devi. These questions mostly related to the disease of a Nai's wife. This Nai had come to Pahalwan Singh Thakur during the *yatra* held during Dussehra. His wife had been assured that her disease would be removed by Deepavali. She had now come to request that her affliction, which had not been cured, be removed.

Local Celebrations—The Melting Pot of Caste Cleavages

Let me mention here that these are the very beliefs and practices which form constituent elements of *shamanism* as recognised in anthropology. The characters that the Parsania villagers call *ghode* or horses are elsewhere known as shamans. While in trance, rural shamans become intermediaries between this-worldly and other-worldly powers. Ordinarily, the roles of a shaman and a priest are quite different and, therefore, some brahmin youths grumbled about 'the superstitions of lower castes' when they saw my interest in this practice. But it is my belief that if the folk culture of Bundelkhand is to be understood, these practices cannot be set aside as superstitions. As mentioned, a large number of the Parsania brahmins participate, in the *maun charana* ceremony as well as the *yatra*. All the elderly people who know the history of the village are agreed that around 1720 AD, one Choube brahmin, one Chamar, one Basor and one Gadaria settled in the village after having migrated from Bhabhua village. Possibly, none of the descendants of the Chamars can now be found in Parsania village. But the descendants of the Choube brahmin, the Basor and the Gadaria are still considered the original settlers or Bhumia, of the village. The celebration of the *yatra* is intrinsically connected to the foundation of this village. This is revealed in two practices. First of all, the Bhumia of the village worship even their own predecessors i.e. the deceased Gond Thakurs of this area. For example, during the month of Kartik, associated with Deepavali, the Bhumia Gadaria and Budhoo went to the shrine of the Gond Thakurs and then made a broomstick of leaves from a Chahor tree and used it in a magical way at the start of the Deepavali celebrations. What I want to emphasise here is that in his capacity as a Bhumia, even a member of the high caste Choube family participates in this celebration in exactly the same way as the lower castes. The other aspect of the brahmins' participation in the *yatra* celebrations is that it is a brahmin priest who conducts the *yagya* and distributes the *prasad*. It is this priest who asks questions of the 'horses'. Nor do the brahmin priests leave the place when the various spirits are seated on their *ghodas*. No. Instead, the priest breaks the coconut and gives pieces of it to all those who have participated in the celebration, irrespective of caste. I, myself, have seen the Brahmin, Kori, Chamar, Ahir, Basor, Gadaria etc.

accepting bits of coconut as *prasad*. Whenever a patient approaches the *ghodas* to pray for a cure, it is the brahmin priest who officiates as an intermediary.

Regional Specificity as a Factor in the Making of History and Society

From the above examples it is clear that the social and religious movements in any specific region of India should be understood within the framework of geographical, political and economic conditions. While, it is true that the idiom of *varna* and *jati* are understood all over India, it is also true that the direction of social change in Indian society cannot be fully understood without taking into account the regional and historical modulations in this process of change. In the Bundelkhand region, the twice born castes (Brahmin, Rajput and Vaishya) are closely tied to their regional milieu. Possibly, the original inhabitants of this region were non-Aryans who inhabited a region where the soil, as compared to that in the Doab, is stony and unproductive. History tells us that this region gave refuge to those brahmins and rulers who were displaced from northern regions. Although, the masses in this area always understood the idiom of kingship, the history of this region has also been one of the rise and fall of ruling houses. Although I cannot deal with this history in detail, a few facts may be mentioned here. It was in this part of Bundelkhand that the Pranami sect flourished. Our research clearly shows that the circumstances in which Chhatrasal Bundela accepted Swami Prannath as his spiritual mentor (*rajguru*) does not amount to the foundation of a sect, which was centuries old and had deep roots in Sanatan Hindu traditions. In fact, the picture which emerges is of a history where a robber today, becomes a king tomorrow. It is also a history where one who is a king today may subsequently lose his authority and have to roam the forests with only a few soldiers. At the same time, there were different kinds of religious beliefs prevailing among the masses. In this milieu, the authority of the king was provided religious sanctity by a chaplain (*rajguru*), whether he was a brahmin or a charismatic sage like Swami Prannath. Not just the towns of Bundelkhand, even in the villages we find shrines of different sects and denominations. All these religious tendencies co-existed and flourished. The constitutions of small princely states even though religious in character, were tolerant of other religions. In states like Chhatarpur, before their integration with the Indian Union, the rulers made donations on all festivals, and affiliates of different religions claimed the gifts and donations through royal patronage. Here we find the kind of religious atmosphere Dr Hazari Prasad Dwivedi describes:

> Indian society has not always been like what it is today. The social organisation today is not an eternal one. In fact the social system of the large masses has always been dynamic. We find that there have been currents in Indian religion which have moved the Indian society from top to bottom. There was a time when a large proportion of the masses in this country did not subscribe to Brahmanical religion. Social groups had their own separate traditions, social organisation and beliefs about the life (Dwivedi 1947; trans. mine).

So far I have dealt mainly with the social conditions of brahmins and Rajputs in eastern Bundelkhand, although I have mentioned the so-called lower castes, and their relations with the upper castes, briefly, in the context of economic and religious traditions. After the Census of 1931, the Indian Government passed a legislation according to which questions regarding caste were banned for census operations. But in the 1911 census of the Central India Agency, which included the princely states of Bundelkhand, the majority population belonged to the brahmin caste, followed immediately by the Chamars. In the decade of the 1950s where, in accordance with the directives of the Constitution, Scheduled Castes and Scheduled Tribes were included in the decennial Census, the population of these categories was exactly one quarter of the total population. The castes included in this category were the Basor, Chamar, Dumar, Kumhar, Bhangi and Beria. Besides these, there were the Ahir,

Kachi, Kori, Dhimar, Lodhi, Kurmi etc. who were also considered shudras but not untouchables. In fact, it is very difficult to give a general account of untouchability among the castes of this second category.

Inter-Caste Reality: A Contravention of the Principle of Ritual Hierarchy

There is also some other evidence that suggests that the specific ranking of the castes in a social hierarchy depended to some extent on the rulers. In Chhatarpur, some barbers had a special relationship with the ruling house. In one of the villages of this kingdom, the Patel or Mukhia belonged to the Basor caste. Those Ahir women who belonged to the Dauwa caste were foster-mothers for Rajput princes and in many villages of the Panna and Chhatarpur states, even today, Dauwa caste people consider themselves 'milk brothers' (*dudh bhai*) of the Rajputs. In the same context, we should also note that among these former princely states, the brahmins acted as priests not only in the rituals of the twice-born castes but also in those of the shudra castes which were touchable. The brahmin priests also accepted gifts from these castes. All the shudras have been firm believers in the path of devotion (*bhakti marg*) according to their own traditions. For example, in Parsania village, the Chamars sing night-long *sakhies* (stories or traditional lores) of Kabir and the songs of Sant Raidas. The tailors belonging to the Darji or Chipi caste are devotees of Namdeo. Dhimars and Kachhis have their own 'Ram' who should be related in this region with Hinduism of the devotional path. All this evidence supports our view that in this milieu, Hinduism has not given a single uniform definition to the various tendencies of folk religion. Each caste retained its special character and this is why the various forms of religion and culture developed and flourished in this region.

Like other regions of India, in Bundelkhand also, the history of the twentieth century, consisting of historical and economic changes, should be seen in this context. One may raise a number of questions: why in rural areas do the twice-born *kisans* continue to dominate? Why is it that the village Panchayats are unable to follow the ideal of welfare for all? Why, despite the democratic aims of the administration, are the dalits and backward classes unable to get their fair share of land? Why is it that despite general elections, it is only the dominant, and traditionally powerful, high caste people who get elected? Why do village leaders ignore ideologies and indulge in political brokerage? What is at the root of bribery and dacoity etc? Instead of answering these questions, I would rather put forward some facts which might inform our understanding of possible future changes.

The contemporary profile of power and dominance:

1. In native states like Chhatarpur, Orchha and Panna, the political agents of the British administration were in place from the beginning of the nineteenth century. In the present century, we find that the Diwans of Chhatarpur state were brahmins who had earlier been officials of the British Government. In this way, gradually, the state administration began to be based on the British model.
2. Since in this area, the brahmins did not enjoy superiority merely on the basis of birth, there was an incentive for them to seek education. On the basis of their traditions and their diplomatic skills, they were able to maintain a high status in the villages. In the villages of Eastern Bundelkhand, brahmin landlords wield guns and are also money-lenders etc. This is proof of the fact that the brahminical traditions of these castes have been overlaid by kshatriya and vaishya traditions. In the populist understanding, the brahmins consider their higher intelligence, education, power and tact the key to their success. At the same time, in order to control the non-brahmin Hindu castes, they also claim championship of the Sanatan Hindu faith.
3. In order to ensure dominance over rural society, it is absolutely essential to control land. Those who possess good land have a higher status. In those villages where a

few twice-born caste households have a monopoly over land, they are known as the houses of '*bhale log*'. In these villages, there is a close relationship between land-ownership, money-lending and agricultural labour (*harwahi system*). The majority population consists of *harwahas* and the minority of landowners. There is an underlying hostility between these two classes. The landlords have many ways in which to extinguish the fire of rebellion among the landless labourers. The truth is that where there is a monopoly of power and resources in the hands of a few wealthy families, a successful rebellion is unlikely. Therefore, the Harijans and backward classes of this region remain subdued. They do their best to come to terms with the dominant castes. This attitude of surrender to the dominant castes is expressed in the saying:

Raha baran ko chahiye, suvidha ek vichar,
Teen cheeje ko khayiye, mahua, ber, achar.

(Live amicably with the influential people of the village, considering that your food consists of products of the jungle i.e. *mahua*, *ber* and *achar*).

Besides brahmin-dominated villages, the other villages in this area can be divided into two categories. These are: the Thakaras villages and those where Ahirs, Kurmis, Koris or Lodhas dominate. In Thakaras villages, some Rajput (Thakur) households have been, and continue to be, influential. Other villages are dominated by the Ahirs, Kurmis, Koris or Lodhas. Without further fieldwork, it is difficult to say what proportion of villages lie in each of these categories in north-eastern Bundelkhand. But conflicts over power and authority occur in all these villages. However, it is my guess that in brahmin-dominated villages, conflicts are usually confined to different factions within the brahmin caste, while in the other two types of villages, there are inter-caste conflicts as well. I am led to this conjecture by the fact that the brahmins—even where they control the social structure—continue to receive gifts i.e. *dan*. Besides, their religious and social tradition considers frugality an ideal. On the whole, one may say that the brahmins have been able to utilise their traditional spirituality, inclusive of the ideal of frugality, and their diplomatic skills, to meet their economic ends. It is probable that only recently have the political battles of the villages in this region come to be fought in the idiom of caste. There is no doubt that the brahmin households have factions, which have resulted from sharp inequalities among the brahmins themselves. But they are still considered controllers of village morality and, therefore, they enjoy not only a superior ritual status, but also wield more power in village politics.

I do not have much experience of Thakaras villages, but my impression is that the Thakur *bhale log* (influential persons) express their leadership over the villages using a kingly idiom. Exhibitionism, ostentatious living, giving away of gifts etc. are a measure of their dominance, control and power. Undoubtedly, their dominance is also based on land ownership, but in addition to this, they also have certain other ideals like strength and arms, display and honour. These values do not go with money-lending. It fact, we can characterise the social, economic and political structure of Thakaras villages as being feudalistic. In the changing economic and political circumstances, their strategy for maintaining dominance is 'distribution' rather than frugality and money-lending. Traditional avenues of maintaining power, e.g. *begar* and taxation are no longer open to the Thakurs. In fact, the dissolution of previous feudal power creates problems not only for the rulers but also for the feudal lords, *jagirdars* and their relatives.

If we compare brahmin *bhale log* with the dominant Thakurs, we find that whereas the brahmins consolidated their hold on material resources, the Thakurs always maintained control over human resources. In democracy, by contrast to monarchy, it is much more difficult and expensive to control human beings. As rural life becomes progressively monetised, and subject to market forces, the Thakurs are now having to pay for human services according to monetary and market considerations. Only those Thakurs who have been able to create businesses out of their landholdings, for example, through mechanisation of farms and ownership of means of transport, continue to be powerful and dominant. Even these individuals are able to maintain their status only to the extent that they are able to distribute their resources by gifts etc. All this requires money, as also does the democratic politics of elections.

Earlier, however, the basis of Thakur prosperity, wealth and power was not money but command (*hukum*). But the price of obedience was security, which was provided by the ruler who did his best to keep the ruled away from harm. Today, these responsibilities have passed on to administrators, even though they are not directly part of rural life. Even now, the leadership of rural village is a contested area, among village dominants. In the eyes of the villagers, the Thakurs should take up leadership roles. In practice, however, only those Thakurs can do so who are able to preserve village norms and at the same time handle market forces and business organisation. The Thakurs of eastern Bundelkhand have solved this problem in three ways. (1) Some of them have mechanised their large landholdings and adopted modern methods of farming to increase their productivity. Along with this, they have been acquiring buses and have shown business acumen as transporters. They are also prepared to take up leadership roles in accordance with the new definitions. (2) Some Thakurs have refused to come to terms with modernity and change despite the fact that they continue to have control over resources and education. This attitude has caused them to jeopardise democratic norms, justice and security. (3) Other Thakurs have tried to limit and restrict their traditional duties.

We know very little about those villages where Ahir, Kurmi, Kori or Lodha are dominant. I believe that a study of these villages would be very helpful in providing answers to questions of caste, clan and tradition in this area. They will provide further evidence of the distinctive social dynamics of this region. The social dynamic of this area has a special atrribute: instead of just the caste system and caste status, there is also group dynamics, and the role of groups may well cut across castes. These groups may provide the units for sociological analysis in this area (cf. Kyung Hak Kim 1994). There are other aspects of contemporary socio-cultural life which hark back to the rich heritage of the history and legends of Bundelkhand. A most interesting area of investigation would be the use of legendary figures for the inventions of memory for political mobilisation especially among the dalit sections of society. For instance, a fruitful area of research would be the evocation of the memory of a figure like Jhalkaribai in contemporary rural areas of Jhansi and thereabouts. Jhalkaribai is portrayed in the current politically charged mythology of the Bahujan Samaj Party (B.S.P.) as a valiant lady who was a member of the *Durga vahini* brigade led by Jhansi Rani Lakshmi Bai of the 1857 rebellion fame (B.N. Tiwari 1998). Another mythology based on the groundswell of collective memory in Bundelkhand refers to the evocations by local scholars and literary persons of socially marginal groups such as the Beria. The Berni or the (religious) prostitutes of Bundelkhand belong to this caste. Alakhnandan, a lecturer in Bhopal, scripted and directed a play on the life and miracles of Chanda Berni and its cosmologically charged interface with kingship (Alakhnandan, n.d.). Sociologically, the ethnography of the Beria community in Bundelkhand is fascinating. For instance, Beria households to this day challenge the traditional north Indian paradigm of patriliny since among them Berni sisters, who are prostitutes, and their children, live jointly with the non-Beria wives and children of their brothers. Women of the latter category are not prostitutes, but ordinary housewives. (cf. Agrawal 1999 for an initial statement).

Conclusion

In conclusion, I would reiterate that in Indian society, the idiom of high and low is dependent on region and context. I believe that the delineation of social structure and dynamics in any region of India should be done in a historiographical manner so that we may be able to formulate objective propositions. We can compare the culture and society of a people with another culture and society only to the extent that we conduct our research in the language with which we are most familiar. In this way, we shall be translating between various societies and cultures and, because we are most familiar with one particular language, it will be possible for us to translate another culture's idiom into our own authentic language. This would be the touchstone of understanding. If this process of research is adopted by social anthropologists, then it is likely that anthropology proceeds towards that truth where the similarities and differences between various human societies and cultures will be captured by a generalised vocabulary and we shall be able to build a new authentic language for cultural translation.

References

Primary Sources

Bundelkhand Agency Records (B.A.R.) Vernacular Files, 1880-1915, Series II. *National Archives*: Delhi.

Kesava Das Misra. 1904. *Birsingh Caritra* (1607 A.D.) (Kasi).

Lal Kavi c.1700. *Chhatraprakasa* (Mss, Hindi) India Office Library: London.

Secondary Sources

Agrawal, Anuja, 1999, *Kinship, Economy and Female Sexuality: A Case Study of Prostitution among the Bedias*. Ph.D. Research Proposal at the Centre for the Study of Social Systems, Jawaharlal Nehru University: New Delhi (mimeographed).

Alakhanandan, N.D. *Chanda Berni: A Play* (Hindi); mimeographed.

Anderson, Benedict 1983. *Imagined Communities: Reflections on the Origin and Spread of Nationalism*. London: Verso.

Baden-Powell, B.H. 1896. *Indian Village Community*. London: Longmans, Green and Co.

Bailey, F.G. 1960. *Tribe, Caste and Nation*. Manchester: Manchester University Press.

Bailey, F.G. 1961. '"Tribe" and "Caste" in India'. *Contributions to Indian Sociology* (Old Series), 5: 7-19.

Bailey, F.G. 1963. 'Closed Social Stratification'. *European Journal of Sociology*, 4(1).

Beteille, A. 1966. *Caste, Class and Power: Changing Patterns of Stratification in a Tanjore Village*. Bombay:Oxford University Press.

Beteille, A. 1974. *Studies in Agrarian Social Structure*. Delhi:Oxford University Press.

Bloch, M. 1971. 'The Moral and Tactical Meaning of Kinship Terms'. *Man* 6, pp. 79-87.

Bohannan, P. 1965. 'The Differing Realms of the Law'. In L. Nader (ed.) *The Ethnography of Law. American Anthropologist* Special Publication, pp. 33-42.

Bosch, F.D.K. 1960. *The Golden Germ: An Introduction to Indian Symbolism*. The Hague: Mouton.

Bose, N.K. 1959. 'Some Aspects of Caste in Bengal'. In Milton Singer (ed.), *Traditional India: Structure and Change*. Philadelphia: The American Folklore Society, pp.191-206.

Burghart, Richard. 1983. 'Renunciation in the Religious Traditions of South Asia'. *Man* (n.5) 18:635-53.

Campbell, George. 1852. *Modern India. A Sketch of Civil Government to which is Prefaced some Account of the natives and Native Institutions.* London: J. Murray.

Carrithers, Michael. 1992. *Why Humans Have Cultures: Explaining Anthroplogy and Social Diversity*. Oxford and New York: Oxford University Press.

Chandra, S. and S.P. Gupta, 1966. 'The Jaipur Pargana Records'. *The Indian Economic and Social History Review*, 3: 3.

Clifford, James and G.E. Marcus (eds.). *Writing Culture: The Poetics and Politics of Ethnography*. Berkeley: University of California Press.

Cohn, B.S. 1962. 'Political Systems in Eighteenth Century India: The Banaras Region, *Journal of the American Oriental Society*, 82: 312-19.

Cohn, B.S. 1965. 'Anthropological Notes on Disputes and Law in India'. In Laura Nader (ed.) *The Ethnography of Law*. American Anthropologist, Special Publication, 67(6), Part 2.

Cohn, B.S. 1969. 'Structural Change in Indian Rural Society, 1586-1885'. In R.E. Frykenberg (ed.) *Land Control and Social Structure in Indian History*. Madison: University of Wisconsin Press. pp. 53-121.

Comaroff, John and Jean. 1992. *Ethnography and the Historical Imagination*. Boulder: Westview Press.

Coulborn, R. 1968. 'Feudalism, Brahmanism, and the Intrusion of Islam upon Indian History'. *Comparative Studies in Society and History*, 10, pp. 357-74.

Crooke, W. 1974. *The Tribes and Castes of North Western India*. 4 vols., repn. Delhi (Original title; *The Tribes and Castes of the North Western Provinces and Oudh*).

Das, V. 1968. 'A Sociological Approach to the Caste Puranas: A Case

Study'. *Sociological Bulletin (Journal of the Indian Sociological Society)*. 17, pp. 141-64.

Drake-Brockman, D.L. 1999. *District Gazetteers of U.P., Vol. XXIV, Jhansi*. Allahabad: Government Press.

Dube, S.C. 1968. 'Caste Dominance and Factionalism'. *Contributions to Indian Sociology* (New Series), 2.

Dumont, L. and Pocock, D.F. 1957. 'Village Studies'. *Contributions to Indian Sociology* (Old Series), 1.

Dumont, Louis. 1960. World Renunciation in Indian Religious. *Contributions to Indian Sociology*, 4: 33-62.

Dumont, Louis. 1964. 'Marriage in India: The Present State of the Question II: Nayar and Newer'. *Contributions to Indian Sociology* (Old Series), 7: 77-98.

Dumont, Louis. 1964. 'Nationalism and Communalism'. *Contributions to Indian Sociology (Old Series)*, 7: 30-70.

Dumont, Louis. 1965. 'The Functional Equivalents of the Individual in Caste Society'. *Contributions to Indian Sociology)*. (Old Series), 8.

Dumont, Louis. 1966. 'Marriage in India: The Present State of the Question III: North India in Relation to South India'. *Contributions to Indian Sociology* (Old series), 9, pp. 90-114.

Dumont, Louis. 1966. 'The "Village Community" from Munro to Maine'. *Contributions to Indian Sociology* (Old Series), 8.

Dumont, Louis. 1967. 'The Conception of Kingship in Ancient India'. *Contributions to Indian Sociology*, 6:48-77.

Dumont, Louis. 1970. *Homo Hierarchicus: The Caste System and its Implications*. London: Weidenfeld and Nicolson.

Dwivedi, Hazari Prasad. 1947, *Hamare Purane Sahitya Ke Itihasa Ki Samagri*. Premi Abhinandan Granth. Allahabad.

Elliot, H.M. 1869. *Memior on the History, Folklore, and Distribution of the Races of the N.W.P. Being an Amplified Edition of the Original Supplemental Glossary of Indian Terms by the late Sir H.M. Elliot*. ed. and revised by J. Beames, London: J. Trubner.

Epstein, S. 1962. *Economic Development and Social Change in South India*. Manchester: Manchester University Press.

Evans-Pritchard, E.E. 1962. 'The Divine Kingship of the Shilluk of the Niltotic Sudan'. In *Social Anthropology and Other Essays*. pp. 192-212, New York: Free Press.

Feeley-Harnik, Gillian. 1985. 'Issues in Divine Kingship'. *Annual Review of Anthropology*, 14, 273-313.

Fox, Robin. 1967. *Kinship and Marriage: An Anthropological Perspective.* Penguin.

Fox, Richard. 1971. *Kin, Clan, Raja, and Rule.* Berkeley: University of California Press.

Franklin, J. 1827. *Memoir of Bundelkhand* (Transaction of the Royal Asiatic Society of Great Britain and Ireland, i. 259-81).

Fried, M.H. 1957. 'The Classification of Corporate Unilineal Descent Groups'. *Journal of the Royal Anthropological Institute.* 87(1). January-June.

Frykenberg, R.E. (ed.). 1969. *Land Control and Social Structure in Indian History.* Madison: University of Wisconsin Press.

Gluckman, M. 1965. *Politics, Law and Ritual in Tribal Society.* Oxford. Basil Blackwell.

Godelier, M. 1965. 'The Notion of the "Asiatic Mode of Production" in Marx and Englse'. *Enquiry* (New Series), 2.

Guha, Ramachandra. 1994. *The Unquiet Woods: Ecological Change and Peasant Resistance in the Himalay.* Delhi: Oxford University Press.

Gupta, B.D. 1958. *Bundelkhand Kesari Maharaja Chhatrasal Bundela.* Agra: Shivlal Agrawal and Co.

Habib, I. 1963. *The Agrarian System of Mughal India* (1556-1707). London: Asia Publishing House.

Hocart, A.M. 1936, 1970. *Kings and Councillors: An Essay in the Comparative Anatomy of Human Society.* Ed. and intro. R. Needham. Chicago: University of Chicago Press.

Hocart, A.M. 1969. *Kingship.* Oxford: Oxford University Press.

Jain, R.K. (ed.) 1971. 'The Anthropological Relevance of Sleeman's *Rambles and Recollections of an Indian Official (1845)*'. Unpublished manuscript of a paper presented to the South Asian History Seminar, Oxford.

Jain, R.K. 1973. 'Review of *Kanbi and Patidar* by D.F. Pocock'. Times Higher Education Supplement. 30 March.

Jain, R.K. 1999. *The Universe As Audience: Metaphor and Community Among the Jains of North India.* Shimla. Indian Institute of Advanced Study.

Kane, I. 1946. *History of Dharmasastra* (Ancient and Medieval, Religious and Civil Law) Vol. III. Poona: Bhandarkar Oriental Research Institute.

Kanhaiyaju, Kunwar. 1928. 'Eka Aitihasika Bhramasansodhana'. *Nagari Pracharini Patrika*, 9: 169-208.

Karve, Irawati. 1968. *Kinship Organisation in India*. Bombay: Asia Publishing House.

Kolff, D.H.A. 1990. *Naukar, Rajput and Sepoy: The Ethnohistory of the Military Labour Market in Hindustan, 1450- 1850*. Cambridge: Cambridge University Press.

Kumar, D. 1962. 'Caste and Landlessness in South India'. *Comparative Studies in Society and History*, 4(3).

Kyung Hak Kim. 1994. *Socio-political Dominance and Segmentation: An Ethnography of Group Dynamics in a Village of Northern Madhya Pradesh*. Unpublished Ph.D Dissertation. Jawaharlal Nehru Univeristy: New Delhi.

Leach, E.R. 1969. 'Introduction: What Should We Mean by Caste?' In E.R. Leach (ed). *Aspects of Caste in South India, Ceylon and North-West Pakistan*. Cambridge: Cambridge University Press.

Luard, C.E. 1907. *Central India State Gazetteer Series, Eastern States (Bundelkhand)*, Vol. VI-A, Text. Lucknow: Newul Kishore Press.

Luard, C.E. 1909. *Bundelkhand Castes* (The Ethnographical Survey of the Central India Agency, Monograph III), Lucknow: The Nawal Kishore Press.

Luard, C.E. (ed). 1928. *Rulers, Leading Families and Officials in the States of Central India*. Calcutta: Government of India, Central Publication Branch.

Madan, T.N. 1998. *Modern Myths, Locked Minds*. Delhi: Oxford University Press.

Maddison, Angus. 1971. *Class Structure and Economic Growth: India and Pakistan since the Moghals*. London: Allen and Unwin.

Maine, H.S. 1871. *Village Communties East and West*. London: J. Murray.

Malcolm, J. 1824. *A Memoir of Central India*. vol.i. London: Parbury, Allen.

Mayer, A.C. 1958. 'The Dominant Caste in a Region of Central India'. *Southwestern Journal of Anthropology*, 14: 407-427.

Mayer, A.C. 1965. *Caste and Kinship in Central India*. London: Routledge and Kegan Paul.

McCall, G. 1971. *Dharma as an Alternatve Concept for Examining Jati and Jajmani Relationship in Village India*. Unpublished B. Litt. thesis: University of Oxford.

Miller, E.J. 1954. 'Caste and Territory in Malabar'. *American Anthropologist*, 56(3).

Monier-Williams, M. 1964. *A Sanskrit-English Dictionary*. New Edition. Oxford: The Clarendon Press.

Moore, Barrington. 1969. *Social Origins of Dictatorship and Democarcy.* Harmondsworth: Penguin.

Pocock, D.F. 1962. 'Notes on Jajmani Relationships'. *Contributions to Indian Sociology.* 6 (Old series).

Pocock, D.F. 1972. *Kanbi and Patidar: A Study of the Patidar Community of Gujarat.* Oxford: The Clarendon Press.

Pogson, W.R. 1828. *A History of the Boondelas.* Calcutta: The Asiatic Lithographic Co.

Rivers, W.H.R. 1921. 'The Origin of Hypergamy'. *Journal of the Bihar and Orissa Research Society,* 8: 9-24.

Roy, Tapti. 1994. *The Politics of a Popular Uprising: Bundelkhand in 1857.* Delhi: Oxford University Press.

Russell, R.V. and Hiralal. 1916. *The Tribes and Castes of the Central Provinces.* Vol. IV. London: Macmillan.

Sengar, Shivnath Singh. 1927. 'Kannauj ke Gaharwaron aur Jodhpur ke Rathoron ki Sajatiyata'. *Saraswati,* 28: 1045-53.

Shah, A.M. 1964. 'Political Systems in Eighteenth Century Gujarat'. *Enquiry,* 1: 83-95.

Sherring, M.A. 1872. *Hindu Tribes and Castes as Represented in Benaras.* London: Trubner.

Silberrad, C.A. 1902. 'A Contribution to the History of W. Bundelkhand'. *Journal of the Asiatic Society of Bengal,* 71: 99-135.

Singh, M.P. 1975. *Aitihasika Pramanavali aur Chhatrasal.* New Delhi: Shripatal Prakashan.

Singh, M.P. (ed). 1973. *Lal-Kavi Krita Chhatraprakasa.* New Delhi: Shripatal Prakashan.

Sleeman, W.H. 1915. *Rambles and Recollections of an Indian Official.* Revised and annotated by V.A. Smith. London: Oxford University Press.

Smith, V.A. 1875. 'Popular Songs of the Hamirpur District in Bundelkhand, N.W.P.' *Journal of the Asiatic Society of Bengal,* LXIV, 384-392.

Smith, V.A. 1881. 'Contributions to the History of Bundelkhand'. *Journal of the Asiatic Society of Bengal,* 60: 1-52.

Tambiah, S.J. 1972. 'From Varna to Caste through Mixed Unions'. In Jack Goody (ed.) *The Character of Kinship.* Cambridge: Cambridge University Press.

Tambiah, S.J. 1973. 'Dowry and Bridewealth and the Property Rights of Women in South Asia'. In Jack Goody and S.J. Tambiah (eds).

Bridewealth and Dowry. Cambridge: Cambridge University Press, pp. 59-169.

Thorner, D. 1956. 'Feudalism in India'. In R. Coulborn (ed). *Feudalism in History*. (Princeton), pp. 133-50.

Tiwari, Badri Narayan. 1998. *Symbol, Memory and Politics: A Social Documentary*. Paper presented at the International Seminar on Popular Culture and Social Action, Pune 2-8 January (mimeographed).

Tiwari, G. 1933. *Bundelkhanda Ka Sankshipta Itihasa*. Kasi: Nagari Pracharini Sabha.

Verma, Vrindavan Lal. 1957. *Garhkundar*. Jhansi: Mayur Prakashan.

Wiser, William H. 1958. *The Hindu Jajmani System*. Lucknow: Lucknow Publishing House.

Index